The Hard Road:

THE ROLLERCOASTER CAREER OF

Atomic Rooster

and Vincent Crane

Marc Shapiro

The Hard Road:

THE ROLLERCOASTER CAREER OF

Atomic Rooster

and Vincent Crane

Marc Shapiro

WP
WYMER
PUBLISHING
Bedford, England

First published in 2025 by Wymer Publishing, Bedford, England
www.wymerpublishing.co.uk Tel: 01234 326691
Wymer Publishing is a trading name of Wymer (UK) Ltd.

ISBN: 978-1-915246-78-3

Edited by Jerry Bloom.

Printed and bound in Great Britain by
CMP, Dorset.

A catalogue record for this book is available from the British Library.

eBook formatting by Lin White at Coinlea Services.
Typeset/Design by Andy Bishop / Tusseheia Creative
Cover design: Tusseheia Creative.

Contents

Introduction: Atomic Who?   9
Chapter One: Enter Vincent Crane   15
Chapter Two: Paying Dues 64-67   19
Chapter Three: The God Of Hellfire   23
Chapter Four: What's In A Name?   31
Chapter Five: Unleash The Rooster   33
Chapter Six: That's Rooster With Three Os   39
Chapter Seven: Palmer Feels The Pressure   47
Chapter Eight: Bring On The Hit   53
Chapter Nine: Trouble In Rooster Land   59
Chapter Ten: Time Is Tight   65
Chapter Eleven: Crash And Burn   75
Chapter Twelve: Made In England: Rest In Pieces   77
Chapter Thirteen: Where Roosters Go: The Early Seventies   93
Chapter Fourteen: Vincent's Head Examined   95
Chapter Fifteen: Wife Number Two   99
Chapter Sixteen: Not Missing In Action   101
Chapter Seventeen: Among Other Things   105
Chapter Eighteen: Did They Do It For The Money?   109
Chapter Nineteen: Rooster Is Snake-Bit   113
Chapter Twenty: Crane Sings While Rooster Burns   117
Chapter Twenty-One: A Curious Side Project   121
Chapter Twenty-Two: A Recipe For Success?   123
Chapter Twenty-Three: If It Wasn't For Bad Luck   127
Chapter Twenty-Four: Just About Midnight   129
Chapter Twenty-Five: It's Great Being Mad   131
Chapter Twenty-Six: The Last Gigs Of Crane On Earth   133
Chapter Twenty-Seven: A Lovely Warm Damaged Man   135
Chapter Twenty-Eight: The Rooster At Rest   137
Chapter Twenty-Nine: They've Come For The Rooster   139
Chapter Thirty: Into The Future   143
Chapter Thirty-one: All Hail The Imperfect Beast   145
Epilogue: Here Comes The Sun   147
Appendices   149
    Discography   149
    They're With The Band   155
    Sources   157
About The Author   159

Introduction
Atomic Who?

The last time Atomic Rooster set foot on US soil was on 24th November 1972, performing in New York as the opening act for their fellow UK counterparts, Savoy Brown. This marked the final performance in a total of eight shows the British band would ever play in America.

During that same peak period between 1970 and 1972, US audiences seeking Atomic Rooster's consistently compelling and electrifying fusion of heavy rock, metal, and blues on vinyl also faced a challenge. Their records were difficult to find, requiring dedicated fans to search far and wide for a copy.

In 1970, their album *Death Walks Behind You* reached a peak position of No. 90 on the US charts. The following year, *In Hearing Of Atomic Rooster* fared poorly, charting at No. 167. Their 1972 release, *Made In England*, did little better, reaching only No. 149.

That would mark both the beginning and the end of Atomic Rooster's American invasion.

Overseas, however, the band fared *light years* better during the same period. Following a largely overlooked — headlining gig at Isle of Ely College, Atomic Rooster benefited from positive word of mouth over their next twenty shows. These included mid-level slots at several outdoor festivals across the UK (and a one-off festival in Germany), sharing line-ups with major acts such as Yes, Black Sabbath, The Who, and Humble Pie. The very same albums that vanished quickly from the US charts enjoyed a much stronger reception at home.

As for drummer Carl Palmer — who to this day insists it was he, not Vincent Crane, who founded the original incarnation of Atomic Rooster before departing for pastures new with Emerson, Lake & Palmer — he has always disputed claims of the band's supposed lack of popularity during his time with them, describing such assessments as highly questionable at best, as he recalled in *T Make World.com*.

"From the beginning, Atomic Rooster was a very big band in Europe. We had an underground following that was huge. It wasn't so big in America. We never really got there. But the band was huge in places like Germany, Italy, France, which was unheard of at the time, and Sweden. We could have worked all the time."

Their debut album, *Atomic Roooster*, reached No. 49 on the UK charts. *Death Walks Behind You* performed notably better, charting at No. 12 in the UK, No. 13 in Australia, and No. 44 in Canada. *In Hearing Of Atomic Rooster* reached No. 18 in the UK and No. 45 in Canada. *Made In England* charted at No. 42 in both Australia and Canada.

Adding to this momentum were a couple of promising singles: 'Tomorrow Night' reached No. 11 in the UK, while 'Devil's Answer' climbed even higher to No. 4. At that point, Atomic Rooster appeared poised for major success in the 1970s hard rock and heavy metal scene.

In what may have been overly exuberant praise, the band was even being talked about as the heir apparent to Cream. Were they really that good? Some argued they were. But then — what happened?

Atomic *Who* is what happened.

First, the good stuff: Atomic Rooster could definitely play. If your tastes lean towards hard progressive rock — dominated by sharp, staccato, probing keyboards and thick, biting guitar riffs — then Atomic Rooster delivered in spades. They were very much in the tradition of bands like Uriah Heep, Deep Purple, and, for those inclined towards deeper cuts, the debut self-titled album by Captain Beyond.

Lyrically, their material was almost entirely dark, introspective, and melancholy. Even the most uplifting of Atomic Rooster songs came inevitably tinged with shades of grey.

But for the time and place, that was exactly the kind of music people craved. It was a magic era for the dark stuff, and Atomic Rooster were right in the thick of it.

From album to album, they could be maddeningly unpredictable — delivering deathly, Sabbath-style dirges one moment, and then veering into heavy soul, funk, or jazz the next. Depending on the level of chaos within the band at any given time — and particularly the often fragile mental state of founding member Vincent Crane — Atomic Rooster could always be counted on to be consistent in their inconsistency. Their albums frequently shifted, sometimes literally from track to track, in mood, tone, musical style, and lyrical depth.

A perfect example of just how diverse Atomic Rooster could be is the album *Made In England*, which flowed seamlessly from hard rock to heavy soul, gospel to hard prog space music — all blended with a generous dose of deep, soulful improvisation. When it came to the good stuff, Atomic Rooster had always delivered in spades.

But then there were all the elements that, while making for great drama — and the kind of madness and inconsistency that fuels rock and roll biographies — rarely lead to happy endings.

Enter Atomic *Who*.

Between the flashes of brilliance and the ever-present potential for greatness lay gaping holes in touring and recording schedules, largely due to the mental instability of founding member Vincent Crane. Under his leadership, Atomic Rooster frequently changed line-ups, often with startling regularity. The reasons ranged from mercenary motives to creative differences and financial difficulties.

One of the more notorious — albeit brief — instances of musicians coming and going was a three-week European tour during August and into September 1980, which featured the presence of legendary drummer Ginger Baker. By that time, Baker was light years removed from his glory days with Cream and was deep in the throes of financial and drug-related turmoil.

His daughter, Nettie Baker, in email correspondence with this author, acknowledged that there wasn't really much to say about her father's involvement with Atomic Rooster.

"In 1980, my dad was living hand to mouth. After his previous band, Energy, collapsed, he took the offer from Atomic Rooster because he was desperate for cash. He didn't think much of the band musically."

Baker barely lasted the full three weeks before — depending on which version of events one believes — he either abruptly quit the band to join space-rock outfit Hawkwind, or, as reported by *The Daily Mail*, "he was sacked by the band because he couldn't keep up."

Crane would frequently take personal leaves of absence due to recurring bouts of depression and other health issues, often leaving highly talented musicians with little choice but to pursue better-paying and more stable opportunities. The constantly shifting musical identity of Atomic Rooster, combined with Crane's unwavering belief that his way was the only way, regularly led to conflict and explosive fallouts. Even when the band managed to hold things together long enough to produce strong material, fate — or the music industry — would often conspire to derail them.

Exhibit A: a much-heralded US tour in support of *Made In England*, which fans believed would finally break the band in the States, was scuppered at the last minute when the band members failed to secure their visas, resulting in the tour's complete cancellation.

The long, strange journey of Atomic Rooster appeared to come to a tragic end when Vincent Crane's battle with mental illness culminated in his suicide — reportedly by ingesting more than 400 painkillers. In most rock and roll tragedies, that would mark the end of the story. But the life and times of

Atomic Rooster is not like most stories.

The Hard Road: The Rollercoaster Career Of Atomic Rooster And Vincent Crane is, in fact, two stories in one.

It is the story of a mad, driven, and immensely talented musician who created a band — Atomic Rooster — in his own musical and emotional image. It is also the story of the many musicians who came and went, the incidents and unexpected dramas that marked their arrivals, departures, and returns.

This is the tale of a band that could have, should have, and — when the stars briefly aligned — *did* fulfil their promise. They created powerful, masterful music and delivered it in an era when there were no rules; it was the rock and roll version of the Wild West, where adventure and misadventure lurked around every corner.

This is the Atomic Rooster story. It starts now.

14

1
Enter Vincent Crane

Carl Palmer was never one to mince words — or, necessarily, to spare anyone's feelings. He could be the strong, silent, all-business type of musician, or, when the moment called for it, biting and direct.

So when the drummer — who had crossed creative paths with Vincent Crane in The Crazy World of Arthur Brown and, for a brief moment, in the first incarnation of Atomic Rooster before moving on to greener pastures with Emerson, Lake & Palmer — was asked about Crane's parents, Tom and Mary Cheesman, he did not hold back.

"I met Vince's parents once," recalled Palmer in an in-depth interview by Colin Harper for *The Afterword*. "They were both very strange people. Both of them looked weird, but they were both super bright. But to meet them on the street, you'd actually think they were backward."

In reality, Tom and Renee (Mary) were both teachers whose intellectual interests ran from liberal to conservative — and often veered into wildly obscure territory. They were known to associate with far-out thinkers and artists, and, at first glance, appeared to be the archetypal radical bohemians living on the fringes of polite society.

But ultimately, the question arose: were Tom and Mary of sound mind?

There had long been speculation that Tom's side of the family had a history of mental illness, which led to some concern when, in late 1942, Renee became pregnant. On 21st May 1943, Vincent Rodney Cheesman was born. By all accounts, the pregnancy and birth were entirely normal.

Vincent's early years are, in hindsight, something of a blur — but given his parentage, they appeared to be relatively normal. As a student at Westminster public school, fragments of information suggest he was extroverted and outgoing, had a casual circle of mates, and was, for the most part, a fairly typical child.

More or less.

There had been early speculation that, owing to the possible history of mental illness on the Cheesman side of the family, there might be some quirks in Vincent's psychological makeup. However, throughout his teenage years, there were no overt signs — aside from an intense early obsession with music in general, and the piano in particular.

As documented in sources such as *The Afterword* and *RockKeyboard.com*, young Vincent would spend hours at the family piano, delving into a sizeable collection of records that included Hot Lips Page and 78s by Louis Jordan. Reports from family and friends suggest that, by his early teens, the music-obsessed youngster had become quite the self-taught boogie-woogie piano player.

In hindsight, if Vincent was obsessed, it seemed — at that stage, at least — to be in a positive way.

Largely through word of mouth that the young Cheesman was developing into a musical prodigy, Vincent secured a scholarship in 1961 to study musical composition and theory at the prestigious Trinity College of Music. Over the course of three years, he earned twin degrees while gaining a clear-eyed understanding of the college, its curriculum, and the professional realities of a music career.

"I caught up with most of the people at Trinity when I was fifteen," Vincent recalled in a *Sounds* interview. "They were going into a career in teaching and not a career in concert performing. I realised that, technically, all I would be was a

50th rate concert artist. But I also realised that I could write music and I thought, 'Well I might as well concentrate on that'."

Despite his reservations about formal music education, Vincent's time at Trinity proved to be highly productive. His writing style continued to evolve, blending elements of classical music with down-home boogie-woogie. He was also gaining a deeper understanding of the complexities of jazz, blues, and what was considered progressive music at the time. Along the way, he discovered the music and distinctive personality of Graham Bond, and by extension, the power and majestic potential of the Hammond organ. It could also be speculated that in Bond, Vincent recognised future personality quirks within himself, mirrored in Graham Bond's own eccentricities.

While juggling a considerable academic workload at Trinity, Vincent gradually began to step into the world of live performance.

As noted on *GarageHangover.com*, his official stage debut took place in 1963 at a local student venue during a set break, where he performed under the moniker of "the loudest piano player in the world." During this period, Vincent was also involved in various jazz and blues-based bands, including *The Vincent Cheesman Trio* (reportedly Vincent's first professional gig in support of Humphrey Lyttelton at The Marquee Club in 1964) and a short-lived blues band that went by both *The Simon Magus Band* and *The Vincent Cheesman Blues Brothers*.

Vincent's childhood friend and poet-musician-in-the-making, Paul Green, recalled in *The Afterword* that even before Vincent graduated from Trinity, he was already very set in his ways. "Vincent was quite the traditionalist. He liked Stravinsky, but after that, he wasn't really interested in too many people. He was into classical and jazz, but only those musicians who, in his opinion, were true craftsmen."

Vincent's early group efforts were ragtag in terms of talent and, with him at the helm, saw frequent line-up changes. In a quote from *The Afterword*, Vincent admitted his impatience, saying, "I was trying different line-ups and wasn't really getting anywhere." But his drive for musical perfection — even at that embryonic stage — was evident, as he reflected on his post-Trinity struggles with *Sounds*.

"When I left Trinity, I tried to get my own groups together, which I think everybody does. But really, it's the last thing you ought to do because you don't really know anybody. Three years at Trinity College and a couple of degrees is no help when you're starting out. I would ring up somebody just to get a gig and they would say 'Do you read music?' and I would say 'No but I've got two degrees' and they would say 'Never mind that, do you read music?'"

2
Paying Dues 64-67

Pete Brown was riding high in the early days of the UK poetry scene, still some years away from achieving legendary status for his songwriting contributions to Cream, when, in 1965, he briefly crossed paths with Vincent Crane. Brown recalled the encounter in *The Afterword*: "Vincent was actually rehearsing with me in a band doing 'jazzy poetry things.'"

It was a loosely knit community, where groups of musicians and poets would come together, collaborate for a time, and then move on to the next project. The vibe at this point in the cultural revolution was free and easy, providing the perfect environment for Crane to experiment and refine his talents. It was a time and place that suited him perfectly, as he thrived in the role of the musical nomad.

Between 1964 and 1966, Crane seemed to drift in and out of various gigs. During this period, he also spent time with a poetry and jazz ensemble called The Word Engine, which, as it turned out, included his childhood friend Paul Green. In *The Afterword*, Green described Crane as "always creative and quite the showman, who, when not playing music, would spend his time creating short, experimental films."

Around 1965, Crane moved in and out of the group J.C. And The Machine, a band that constantly shifted its musical style, moving from jazz to soul to pop and back again. This period largely went unnoticed, even by the band's own members.

Machine saxophonist Bob Downes later recalled in *GarageHangover.com* that he remembered Crane being in the band for a time but couldn't pinpoint when. The general consensus seemed to be that the keyboardist joined and left during a perceived high point on 4th May 1965, when J.C. And The Machine opened for The Spencer Davis Group.

Although the gig went largely unnoticed, it was believed that this first encounter with the workings of big-time pop music and the music business had a lasting effect on Crane's impressions of both the pop world and what it could offer.

It is also worth noting that, figuratively and literally, this was when the young musician's phone began to ring.

Word had spread through the music scene, and the flamboyant young keyboardist quickly became in demand. His sudden popularity, even for gigs that often lasted only weeks, indicated that Crane was beginning to build a reputation. For him, the seemingly endless search for paying gigs would continue. Talent and the constant need to make ends meet had already become deeply ingrained.

The cycle of fleeting engagements continued after J.C. And The Machine, including stints with Lew Hird's Australian Jazz Band (which included a brief tour of France). Paul Green would later recount in *The Afterword* what might have been Crane's first signs of emotional struggles.

"Something happened on that tour. Vincent returned in a very strange state of mind. The story was that Vincent went berserk at one point on the tour and deliberately flooded the band's hotel. Some people interpreted this as simply rock and roll hijinks. But I wonder if he was, at that point, just plain out of control."

Next on Crane's gig list was a band called The Big Sound and a series of promising demos that ultimately went nowhere, followed by his own groups, Vincent Crane's Freedom Riders and The Vincent Crane Combo. The latter resulted in what could be described as a semi-residency at a club called The Witch's Cauldron.

Reports suggest that Crane approached his music and the process of learning the ropes with a completely professional attitude, even under the most challenging circumstances and when playing gigs that he considered beneath him.

However, even those who recognised and admired his early musical acumen could sense that his ego, coupled with the erratic nature of his mental state, was often teetering on the edge. This would explode once again during a brief engagement with a pop group called Hedgehopper's Anonymous, a one-hit wonder that was sliding into obscurity due to line-up changes, failed follow-up singles, and rapidly declining popularity.

Crane was more than capable musically, but as he shared in *Sounds*, he was still somewhat mercenary in his approach: "I thought they were going to do some cabaret things just to make a bit of money."

Band member Glenn Martin recalled in *The Strange Brew. com*: "I remember Vincent did a couple of gigs with us, and I remember him for one specific incident that nearly got us all killed. We were playing a gig in London, in a docklands area, and halfway through the performance, this woman got up on stage and started doing a striptease. All the dockers in the audience started clapping. Vincent got really upset, saying 'This is disgusting!' He got off his keyboards and just walked out. I thought we were going to get murdered by the crowd. We ended up doing a drum solo over the striptease."

Despite his emotional outbursts, Crane's musical ability earned him a good reputation, which led to several opportunities throughout 1967. Reportedly, he was even recruited by a hitherto unknown group called The Foundation, who would go on to have a number of pop/soul hits. However, Crane declined the offer and ultimately found himself in a musical situation that reflected his mental state at the time.

22

3
The God Of Hellfire

Crane's first brush with stardom came as part of The Crazy World of Arthur Brown and the maddening, psychedelic rock anthem 'Fire.' As recounted by Brown and Crane in sources like *Sounds*, *Psychedelic Baby Magazine*, *Psychedelic Scene*, and others, this is how The Crazy World was born.

"I arrived back in London after a tour in Paris, which had been my first professional engagement," recalled Brown. "I moved into this Bohemian lodging place, and as it turned out, the landlady's daughter was going out with a keyboard player who lived upstairs. Lo and behold, I began to hear this magnificent piano music coming from upstairs. So, I went up to introduce myself, and there was Vincent Crane."

The pair quickly hit it off, despite the contrast in their approaches — Brown, with his theatrical style, and Crane, whose focus was solely on music. But times were tough for struggling musicians (often earning five bob on a good night), and as Crane recalled, he and Brown soon teamed up for their first gig together — a test run of what was to become the progressive rock movement, in a club in Brighton.

That first gig, as chronicled by drummer Drachen Theaker in *The Afterword*, went like this: "It was basically Vincent doing his keyboard set with Arthur squawking over him, coming out in a variety of different costumes and behaving like a maniac."

Ever the perfectionist, Crane was initially unimpressed by Brown's theatrics, as he reflected in *Sounds*: "I wasn't too keen on what he was doing. It was very different from what I was doing, but I knew he was going to be big. I didn't really like what he was doing at the time, but I realised it would be sensible to go with him."

On the surface, Crane's decision to join forces with Brown seemed like an odd pairing. Crane, who was deeply invested in music as a tool for arrangement and song structure, contrasted sharply with Brown, the more flamboyant, theatrical figure, drawing on mystical, classical, soul, and jazz influences. However, these were different times in the UK pop music scene, where it was permissible to experiment, fail, or succeed in opening doors to something new. From the start, it seemed there was room at the cultural table for both of them.

For Crane, who had previously maintained a low-key public persona, the sudden shift was a shock to the system. The normally studious and isolated musician was jolted by the fast-paced nature of the pop music scene. With the addition of drummer Drachen Theaker, the now-christened The Crazy World of Arthur Brown embarked on a rigorous touring schedule throughout 1967 and into 1968, debuting at venues such as The 7½ Club and The UFO Club, alongside a demanding series of gigs — more than Crane had seen in a long time.

It was during these early days with The Crazy World of Arthur Brown that Crane officially adopted his stage name, reportedly derived from Brown's early stage effect, in which he was lowered onto the stage by the titular mechanism.

The band's growing popularity soon caught the attention of none other than guitarist Pete Townshend, who was acting as a de facto talent scout for The Who's fledgling record label, Track Records. As a result, The Crazy World of Arthur Brown fell under the management of the hip music impresario Kit Lambert, who wasted no time testing the waters with the band's first single (and Crane's first arranging credit), 'Devil's Grip.' This track, a blend of rock, psychedelia, and dark imagery, despite some endearing pop sensibilities, failed to chart.

Undeterred, Lambert pushed the band into the studio to record their now-legendary album *The Crazy World of Arthur Brown*, which would later produce the iconic single 'Fire.'

For Crane, who would receive songwriting credits on eight

of the album's ten tracks, it became a gruelling process of fourteen-hour days spent mixing and arranging. He was even tasked with unexpectedly arranging a horn passage to cover what, after the recording, were determined to be weak spots in the drumming on some of the tracks.

As it turned out, the recording session — and the unexpected nature of creating 1960s pop — suited the keyboard player perfectly. He had no trouble embracing spontaneity and quickly demonstrated his ability to combine his more methodical musical style with the demands of crafting three-minute pop songs that would be suitable for radio and resonate with teenage angst.

The album and single were released in June 1968, and the success was immediate. 'Fire' soared to No. 1 on the UK charts in August, and perhaps most notably, it reached No. 2 on the US Billboard charts. The single went on to chart in the top ten of more than half a dozen countries worldwide.

The band, no pun intended, was suddenly "on fire" — the pop flavour of the moment. Crane was about to experience the madness that accompanied having an international hit.

The Crazy World of Arthur Brown quickly set out on their first US tour to capitalise on the immense success of 'Fire' and their album The Crazy World of Arthur Brown. The first leg of the tour, which began in May, saw the band opening for rock royalty such as Jefferson Airplane, The Doors, Jimi Hendrix, and The Who.

No doubt, the publicists concocted whatever they could to guarantee column inches, and Tony Palmer, writing for the UK's *Observer*, was either caught up in it or privy to the hype. His *Pop* column reported: "The Crazy World of Arthur Brown has seemed to some like an absurd, malicious joke. With Vincent Crane on organ and Drachen Theaker on drums, Arthur Brown — vocalist, magician, ex-petrol pump attendant — is now screaming and thundering his way across America with devastating results. In Detroit, three men ran from the ballroom where he was performing, convinced he was the devil; in Miami, the police stopped the show, saying it was 'harmful' to young people. His act, said the *International Times*, is 'the all-time high in erectile music.'"

The tour was a coming-of-age experience for Crane. He absorbed the rock and roll excesses like a sponge, partaking in many of them. Stories abound that it was on this tour that Crane embarked on a drug-taking odyssey, especially with LSD. Prolonged exposure to the drug's effects during the tour only served to exacerbate his increasingly erratic mental state.

By June 1968, The Crazy World of Arthur Brown was already on shaky ground, despite the positive response and the opportunity to hang out with some of the most popular bands on the planet. Crane, in an *The Afterword* piece, reflected on that first US tour: "We were in a position where you would think nothing could go wrong. But by the time we got to the US, the whole thing seemed to be mistimed."

Depending on the source, drummer Drachen Theaker either quit or was fired from the band mid-tour on 5th May, reportedly due to nervous exhaustion. This was partly caused by his fear of flying and the immense pressure of sudden stardom that seemed to be weighing heavily on the band.

The latter appeared to be a key factor during an 11th May concert, when Crane unexpectedly had a meltdown, attacking both Brown and replacement drummer Jeff Cutler on stage. He had to be physically restrained. Brown, in interviews with *Psychedelic Baby Magazine* and *Songfacts.com*, saw Crane's decline as the result of a double-edged personality.

"Vincent had an intelligence that was brilliant. But he would undercut himself when depression of a bipolar nature came on him."

For a time, Crane, according to Brown, was able to manage his depression with medication. However, during one point in the US tour, he inexplicably stopped taking his meds. The situation worsened when, at one stage, he was unknowingly spiked with LSD.

The first leg of the US tour effectively came to a crashing halt, just twenty-four hours after Carl Palmer was officially named the band's permanent drummer. Crane suffered a complete mental breakdown, returned to England, and spent four months in a mental institution, where he was treated for manic depression. During this period, Brown, who had recently married and was staying at a commune for four months, began to formulate plans for a reconfigured line-up and a new musical direction.

Crane eventually returned to The Crazy World of Arthur Brown and, for all intents and purposes, was able to perform again later in 1968, back in England, where he appeared to be in fine form.

At the Nottingham University Rag Ball on 29th October, Tony Willmett was positive about the performance for the *Nottingham Guardian Journal*, stating, "Arthur Brown used all the tricks in the book to mesmerise his audience. His frenzied gyrations and ringing voice took the lead over the organ, bass, and drums accompaniment on 'Spell On You.' The group's organist, twenty-five-year-old Vincent Crane, displayed his considerable potential in the improvised 'Spontaneous Apple Creation,' playing both rhythm and lead."

Just before the show, Brown told Willmett, "Vincent is fantastic on the organ, and we aim to highlight his talent by expanding our line-up to thirteen soon, including violin and cello."

A third US tour began in 1969. Prior to a show at the War Memorial Auditorium in Fort Lauderdale on 2nd April, the band found themselves on the wrong side of the law.

An incident had occurred two nights earlier at the Holiday Inn, where the band had put on an impromptu performance. They trained powerful lights on a building across the street from their motel room and began performing for the visiting college students below.

The spectacle attracted a crowd of around 2,000 cheering students, most of whom spilled into the intersection of Las Olas Boulevard and Atlantic Avenue, a scene reminiscent of the film *Where The Boys Are*. As they watched, Crane danced in front of the lights, casting a huge, ghostly image on the building next door, at which point the police intervened.

Arthur Brown, Vincent Crane, bassist Dennis Taylor, and four backstage workers were all charged with disorderly conduct. Each was released from the city jail on $50 bail.

As it turned out, Crane and Palmer got along well and formed an immediate bond during the tour, and everything seemed right in the world — until June 1969, when both Crane and Palmer left the band. Reportedly, Brown's unexpected commune adventure was the deciding factor in their departure.

For his part, Brown had a different perspective on the unravelling of that incarnation of The Crazy World of Arthur Brown, particularly regarding the departure of Crane and Palmer.

In a *Songfacts.com* interview, Brown revealed that by the time Crane had returned, a very tempting offer was being dangled in front of him by label mogul Clive Davis. However, for reasons that remain unclear to this day, Brown turned down the offer, which, in turn, upset Crane and Palmer so much that they promptly left the band over the major opportunity being discarded.

Palmer recalled their predicament in *The Afterword*. "Arthur had gone off with his wife to a commune in New Jersey. We did manage to locate him but he just wouldn't pick up the phone. So, the two of us were stuck in New York and waiting."

But it would not be a totally unproductive wait.

Crane had been working on new material that could easily have worked for either a tentative new group or for The Crazy World of Arthur Brown. As he later explained in *Sounds*, both Palmer and he were eager for a change and were thinking in terms of a Plan B.

"Carl was hesitating about the whole situation because he wanted to leave, and I wanted to leave. But we weren't sure if the other was thinking the same way. In the end, we made some calls across the Atlantic to see about lining up a bass player."

For completists, Brown saw the dissolution of the current line-up as an opportunity to enter the studio with a new array of musicians, with the exception of Theaker. He emerged with what would become his passion project: a second album, *Strangelands*. The album was a completely avant-garde effort and, not surprisingly, entirely non-commercial. The band's label was unimpressed and shelved *Strangelands*, which would not be released until 1980.

Strangelands would be of small consequence to Crane and Palmer who, by the time the album was dead on arrival, had already packed their bags, paid their hotel bills and were on their way back to England.

4
What's In A Name?

Even before they arrived in the UK, and long before there was a physical band, they had already christened themselves Atomic Rooster.

According to Palmer, as he recounted in *The Afterword*, the whole thing stemmed from an intervention of sorts in a New York apartment before the musicians returned to England.

"We went to this girl's apartment. We took Vincent to see her because she was going to explain how bad acid was and why he (Vincent) should stop taking it. The person she chose to talk about was the bass player for a US band called Rhinoceros, who had taken a lot of chemicals and started calling himself 'the Atomic Rooster.' I couldn't help but laugh at that. It was a great name. When we got back to England, I said to Vincent, 'Why don't we call our band Atomic Rooster? You're never going to become it...'"

'But we could all be part of it,' Vincent replied."

5
Unleash The Rooster

Professionally and personally, things moved quickly in the sixties. Music was created, inspired, and interpreted almost instantaneously. The same applied to personal lives and relationships.

So, it came as no surprise that, shortly after The Crazy World of Arthur Brown had established some semblance of a residency at the UK's Middle Earth Club, sparks flew the moment Crane laid eyes on Pat Darnell.

Very little was known about Darnell, who, as described in *Record Collector Magazine*, worked at the club and was often referred to as 'The Acid Queen'. Details of their courtship are scarce, but Pat's presence in Crane's life would, within a year, appear to have a significant impact on the dark and often ego-driven nature of the musician's mental state.

According to those within the band's inner circle, Pat's growing interest in the spiritual aspects of Wicca began to cast a shadow of witchcraft over Crane, whose mental state had already shown an affinity for the so-called dark arts.

Despite the warning signs, by the time Crane and Palmer left The Crazy World of Arthur Brown and returned to the UK, Crane and Darnell were husband and wife.

The responsibility of marriage was just one of the pressures weighing on Crane at the time. Starting a new creative venture was another, and his ongoing experimentation with LSD added further strain. The result was another mental breakdown, not long after their return to the UK, which led to a second stint in a mental institution.

This left the practical work of forming a new band to Palmer.

By the time Crane was released from the mental hospital, Palmer had secured management through the powerful Robert Stigwood Organisation. The next step was to finalise the Atomic Rooster line-up.

Neither Crane nor Palmer was keen on the traditional bass, guitar, drums, and vocals setup. They ultimately agreed that *Atomic Rooster* should mirror the line-up of The Crazy World of Arthur Brown — keyboards, drums, vocals, and ideally, a bass player who could also sing. However, when the question of adding a guitar was raised, Crane firmly rejected the idea on creative grounds.

"I was reluctant to use guitar at that point because I hadn't really heard anybody who I felt used the guitar the way I felt it should be used in the songs I was writing at the time," Crane offered in a *Sounds* conversation.

Filling out the initial Atomic Rooster line-up was easier said than done.

It began with the recent departure of Rolling Stones' member Brian Jones, who was found dead the day before he was due to meet with Crane and Palmer. The search continued through major figures such as Jack Bruce, Ric Grech, John Paul Jones, and Greg Ridley — all notable musicians in various famous bands throughout their careers. Ultimately, Crane and Palmer turned to musicians' wanted adverts in publications like *Melody Maker* to fill the spot. Palmer, in *The Afterword*, summed up weeks of street auditions:

"It was really bad," he groaned. "Steve Howe (who would later make his mark in Yes) came along, and we thought he was rubbish. Finally, Nick Graham turned up, sang one song, and played some flute."

Palmer and Crane were sold, and Atomic Rooster was born.

From the outset, Atomic Rooster had plenty of street credibility and business backing.

With Robert Stigwood managing them, several doors were immediately opened. Crane and Palmer's previous work with The Crazy World of Arthur Brown added significant pedigree, and they were able to secure gigs, largely based on the curiosity factor alone. Rehearsals with the now-finalised prog rock trio went well. Creatively, Atomic Rooster was on track, with Crane handling the lyrics and melody of original material, while Palmer, largely under the radar, proved solid in song arrangement.

Now all that remained was that all important first gig. A "warm-up" show was played at the Fishmonger's Arms pub in Wood Green, North London on 22nd August 1969. Another show was played at London's Speakeasy on 28th August.

Misleadingly, the posters for the gig at The Lyceum on 29th August 1969 advertised it as Atomic Rooster's first performance. It's likely, however, that the posters were printed before other shows had been scheduled. Atomic Rooster headlined a multi-band bill that also featured Deep Purple — who had just undergone a line-up change — and beat poet/rocker Pete Brown's latest group, Piblokto.

One thing was certain: with Crane rapidly assuming the role of bandleader, Atomic Rooster were punctual. The one thing the often-dictatorial musician would not tolerate was lateness.

ARTHUR BROWN SOLO PLAN =and Atomic Rooster is born!

ARTHUR BROWN has re-signed a management contract with Kit Lambert and Chris Stamp, co-managers of the Who and Thunderclap Newman. He is this week beginning rehearsals as a solo artist backed by an orchestra. "We will work on a change of image and start recording as soon as possible," a spokesman for Track Records told the NME.

Meanwhile, two ex-members of Crazy World of Arthur Brown — which broke up in New York six months ago — have formed a new group to be known as the Atomic Rooster. They are organist and part-composer of "Fire," Vincent Crane, and drummer Carl Palmer. Third member of the team is Nick Graham (bass, flute and vocals).

The group is to make its debut next Thursday (28) at London Speakeasy, and is already booked for a lengthy string of club and college dates, including London Lyceum Midnight Court (29), Plymouth Vandyke (September 1), Hampstead Country Club (7), London Marquee (12), Manchester Magic Village (13), Southampton Concrod (25), Birmingham Mothers (28) and Croydon Star (29). Its debut LP will be issued by Polydor next month.

The band's first tour ran through to 21st December. With prog rock on the rise, Atomic Rooster were already being hailed as the next big thing — even in those early UK gigs.

At least according to Palmer, who acknowledged the band's good fortune: "We did incredibly well that first year. It was like falling out of bed. We had shows where we played in front of 1,500 people. And it was all word of mouth."

But those early shows were also sometimes a struggle. On 6th October they played the Bath Pavilion. They would first have preferred to have played university or college dates in the area before playing a date at the Pavilion. They also failed to understand why the promoter had linked their name with that of Arthur Brown in the publicity, considering the fact that the hall was more than half empty for the Fire man at a time when his record was top of the charts.

But needless to say, the local press were clearly interested in the Arthur Brown angle. The *Western Daily Press* asked Vincent Crane what had happened to Arthur Brown.

"No one really knows," said Crane. "France, maybe. He was very big over there, and he had been record-wise, and he had dreams of making a triumphant entry into France, but I think he has left it too late."

"I could never understand why we never worked there considering he could speak perfect French. Trouble with Arthur was that there was so much talk in his act, he was probably afraid that Europeans wouldn't understand what he was up to."

"Of course, the main problem was that he could not follow up his number one record. That's why we wouldn't want a number one for Atomic Rooster."

A December show at the Toby Jug in Tolworth was reviewed by the *Cobham News and Mail*: "And what a performance! Strangely enough, it was their last-but-one number which really set the place alight — figuratively speaking, of course. A quite unbelievable drum solo, lasting at least ten minutes, followed a virtuoso performance on organ, the sound being completed by the voice and playing of the bass guitarist. He was equally at home playing the flute and, in fact, one of the most pleasing numbers was 'Winter', which depended heavily on the sound of the flute."

Early on, it was Crane who emerged as the leader of the band — both creatively and on the business side. His drive and ego were on constant display, which was perfectly fine with Palmer, who acknowledged as much in an interview with *Sounds*: "Vincent was on a bit of an ego trip at the time, which was okay with me. I let it go as long as I got the money. I got what I wanted, which was the recognition as a drummer."

6
That's Rooster With Three Os

By the time 1969 was drawing to a close, the writing was on the wall: Atomic Rooster was a band on the rise and going places. Their calls were being returned promptly, and gigs were pouring in like raindrops. In short order, they were on top of the world.

"The phone hasn't stopped ringing," enthused Crane in a *New Musical Express* interview at the time. "Things were definitely on top for the band. In fact, we had more than enough work. But one thing was for certain — we were not going to fall into the trap of out-pricing ourselves like so many other bands."

Playing gigs at reasonable rates wasn't Atomic Rooster's only strength. It was clear they were a band that took rehearsals seriously. By progressive rock standards, they were impressively tight as live performers. Add to that the fact that Atomic Rooster were always punctual for gigs, and you got the distinct impression that this was a band ticking all the right boxes.

By December 1969, it became evident that the next step in building on Atomic Rooster's promising momentum was to record their debut album. With tongue perhaps firmly in cheek, the album — *Atomic Roooster* (not a typo) — was recorded at lightning speed between December 1969 and January 1970

MALVERN
WINTER · GARDENS
ATOMIC
ROOSTER
KEITH RELF'S
RENAISANCE
SAT. 1 NOV.
8·30~11·45

and released in February through B&C Records.

"I predict we have another Cream on our hands," was the confident statement from Robert Masters, Director of the Robert Stigwood Organisation.

In February, *Beat Instrumental* said: "Vincent Crane, with various degrees in music, is organist and musical brain behind the Rooster."

The magazine also reported on one of the other musicians Crane and Palmer had initially approached — Ric Grech — as a potential bassist. However, he had already committed to Blind Faith. So instead, they found their "unknown": Nick Graham, then an apprentice engineer who shared their musical tastes. The trio locked themselves away in an East End pub for a couple of months before emerging to hit the road and record an album.

Despite the buzz, they were quick to dismiss comparisons to Cream. "Our music can't really be defined, and we don't want it to be. Like most musicians, we dislike this trend for slapping labels on music," said Vincent and Carl when they spoke with *Beat Instrumental* in the familiar surroundings of Denmark Street — the mecca for musicians in the late sixties and early seventies.

"About the only thing we can say about our music is that a lot of it is based on negro rhythms with something new slapped on top. We try and keep everything reasonably simple and direct, while still retaining a high standard of musicianship. On stage, we're aggressive and forceful; we try to whip up an atmosphere — and we seem to be succeeding. We're aiming at entertainment. Many ordinary people can't grab difficult riffs, but they can sing and dance to the simpler stuff. Apathy in an audience is about the worst thing in the world, so we try and make the audience feel as if they are part of the music — as if they've contributed something to it."

It was one thing to engage an audience during a live performance, but quite another to capture that same energy on record. "On the album, we've tried to make the numbers build up to a sort of climax, with each one progressing from the previous, rather than just an odd assortment of songs thrown together any old how. We want both sides to be the best we can do, so that people will want to play them both."

They also made it clear that their commitment to the band went beyond commercial success. "If we were the biggest flops of all time, we'd still play just for the kick we get out of it. It's in our souls, man."

Ahead of the album's release, *Melody Maker* reported that a four-week tour of the States was under negotiation for March. Meanwhile, their second Swedish tour was set to commence on 3rd February, running for two weeks, followed by a week in Denmark. After that, on 25th February, they were scheduled to head to Germany for two days of television appearances.

But perhaps the most intriguing detail in the *Melody Maker* report was that, before all of that, the band was scheduled to perform at the Lanchester Festival in Coventry on 30th January, and that they had composed a special ten-minute piece, 'Malleus Malesicarum,' specifically for the occasion.

As a relatively new band, Atomic Rooster received little coverage in relation to the festival, but *Melody Maker* journalist Chris Welch was in attendance. In the following week's issue, he wrote: "Atomic Rooster are a fine band. Vincent Crane is an entertaining madman at the organ and Carl Palmer's drumming is remarkable. But they could benefit from less volume. 'Winter', the least thrashing, is their best number."

Atomic Roooster was a promising debut — an immediately enticing slice of progressive rock, guided by Crane's often autobiographical lyrics drawn from his experiences with mental decline, and enriched with ambitious jazz and classical arrangements. The album paid clear homage to Crane and Palmer's time with The Crazy World of Arthur Brown, not least in its blistering cover of John Mayall's 'Broken Wings.'

Early on, the album made it evident that, while Crane was widely seen as the band's driving musical force, he was notably generous in sharing songwriting credits. This was reflected in Palmer and Graham's co-writing credits on the tracks 'Banstead' and 'Decline And Fall.'

Atomic Roooster reached a respectable No. 49 on the UK album charts, coinciding with the release of their debut single

'Friday The 13th.' Although the single failed to chart and the album struggled in overseas markets, it marked a solid foundation for the band's future.

Beat Instrumental reviewed it favourably: "An exciting and powerful first album from a group who have been building up a solid reputation for themselves on the club/college circuit. The Atomic trio are a tight and attacking band who put their music across with force and precision. Carl Palmer's drum work is fast and sharp."

"Vincent Crane continues to pound some amazing sounds from his organ, and Nick Graham does the honours on bass. Their compositions are unequally structured, suggesting his classical training, and are sometimes reminiscent of his work with Arthur Brown, but this is still a mighty first egg from the rooster."

Concerning the single, *The Northern Echo* reported on 12th March, the day before its release, "When the Crazy World of Arthur Brown split, it wasn't the legendary Phoenix that rose from the ashes. It was a Rooster — and an Atomic one at that. But this bird didn't try a get-rich-quick flap round the clubs. For eight weeks they locked themselves away for solid rehearsal, and now after twelve months playing together they have something to crow about."

"At last, the Atomic Rooster trio are satisfied with one of their songs to allow it to be released. And flying in the face of superstition they are releasing 'Friday The 13th' tomorrow."

Crane explained to the paper why it had taken them so long before the first release. "I have seen so many bands rush out a record to capitalise on their success in the clubs and all make the same mistake. We wanted the people who asked for a record to be sure that they were getting something representative of all of us."

The Northern Echo said of 'Friday The 13th', "Fast, loud and original, it has the same urgency of 'Fire' that gives it a definite hit tag."

A few weeks after the release of *Atomic Roooster*, the first in a series of band shake-ups — an ongoing theme throughout much of the band's career — occurred when vocalist and bass

FRIARS
WALTON ST.
AYLESBURY
ANDY DUNKLEY
OPTIC NERVE
ATOMIC
ROOSTER
15 SEPT.
BLOSSOM
TOES 22 SEPT.

player Nick Graham suddenly quit. Reportedly, he was unable to cope with the band's demanding touring schedule.

In the meantime, positive press surrounding both the band and the album was beginning to spread to the United States, and a deal for *Atomic Roooster* to be released there was under negotiation. The only stumbling block appeared to be the perception — accurate or not — that American audiences wanted more guitar in their music. The band took the hint and brought in John Du Cann, a rising guitarist with raw rock and roll sensibilities, to overdub straightforward rock riffs onto several of the album's original tracks.

On the surface, Du Cann's arrival seemed like a smart move. His attitude fit the band's ethos, he had strong guitar skills, and he showed promise as a songwriter. Things seemed to be falling into place for Atomic Rooster.

However, despite the effort, the deal for US distribution of the *Atomic Roooster* album ultimately fell through.

7
Palmer Feels The Pressure

Despite *Atomic Roooster* failing to secure US distribution and making little chart impact outside the UK, Atomic Rooster emerged in the early 1970s as both a critical and fan favourite on the international stage. Palmer confirmed as much in a conversation with *Record Collector Magazine*: "The band had an amazing cult following in places like England, Germany, Sweden and Italy."

Sensing a bright future ahead, Atomic Rooster returned to the studio to record a demo for the track 'Tomorrow Night', which — on first listen — had all the creative hallmarks of a top-ten hit. It was at this promising juncture that Palmer received a phone call most musicians could only dream of — an offer to join Keith Emerson and Greg Lake in a major label project that already had "supergroup" written all over it.

If Palmer agreed, the band would be christened Emerson, Lake & Palmer. However, Palmer was a principled man — a rarity in the pop music world — and, as chronicled by *Record Collector Magazine*, *The Afterword*, *New Musical Express*, *Sounds*, *Musoscribe.com*, and *Drummerworld.com*, things quickly became complicated.

"When I was originally called up by Emerson and Lake's representative with the offer, I said no. Rooster was the first band I had ever formed (with Crane), and I wanted to go a bit

TOMORROW NIGHT
ATOMIC ROOSTER
ESSEX MUSIC INTERNATIONAL LIMITED
20p

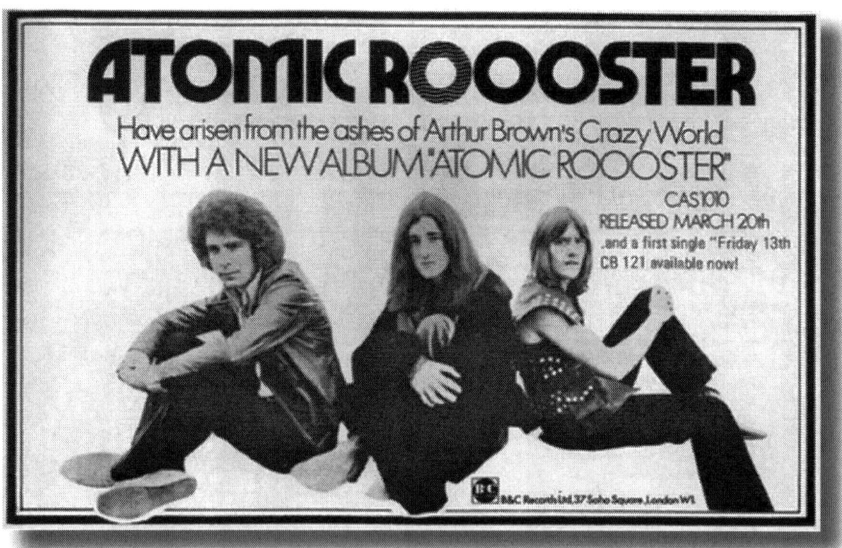
ATOMIC ROOOSTER
Have arisen from the ashes of Arthur Brown's Crazy World
WITH A NEW ALBUM "ATOMIC ROOOSTER"
CAS 1010
RELEASED MARCH 20th
...and a first single "Friday 13th
CB 121 available now!
B&C Records Ltd, 37 Soho Square, London W1

further with it. I also liked the idea of being in a relatively small group. I thought I must give it a bit longer."

Palmer also had a vested business interest in Atomic Rooster—namely, contracts—which made leaving problematic. "There were several contracts I had personally signed because I ran the band, so I had to say no. When the guy who is kind of leading the band decides to leave, it can get a bit dicey."

Nevertheless, Emerson and Lake remained persistent in their pursuit of Palmer.

The pursuit of Palmer quickly escalated to a new level when he was informed that none other than record company mogul Ahmet Ertegun, who was overseeing the formation of what was being discussed as the next big thing, wanted to speak with him.

"Ahmet Ertegun said, 'What would it take? What would you need?' I said I have commitments with Atomic Rooster. If I don't fulfil them, there will be consequences for the band, and I don't want the guys to be held to ransom."

The courtship of Carl Palmer continued when Greg Lake called and invited him to come down to a studio to jam with himself and Keith Emerson.

"I did it and enjoyed playing with them. Greg called again and asked what I was going to do about the situation. I told him I didn't know and needed to think about it. He said he'd call the next day and wanted me to give him an answer. But then he called the same night and suggested we have another rehearsal. At that point, I still said no, but then Greg laid it on the line about how big he thought the band would be. Finally, it all just clicked, and I said yes."

But there were certain terms.

For the next two months, Palmer alternated between playing out the string of dates with Atomic Rooster, averaging five shows a week, and rehearsing three days a week with ELP.

"I found Vincent a replacement drummer in Ric Parnell (who would soon be replaced by Paul Hammond after a couple of months) and settled all the outstanding business matters. I also helped out with the final mix for 'Tomorrow Night' and assisted Rooster as best I could."

ATOMIC ROOSTER
8-00 TILL 1-00
HAWK WIND COLLEGE OF ART ALL
SAINTS WED 28 JAN, 1970 DISCO

MAIDSTONE COLLEGE OF ART
Oakwood Park
FRI., 13th MARCH, 8 p.m.-1 a.m.
ATOMIC ROOSTER
SHADES
GIN HOUSE
WOODEN WORM
Light Show, Disc Jockey—Theo Loyla
Tickets 8/-, 10/- Door
Also at John Kent Boutique
Gooses Record Shop, Art College
Artists booked through —
Peter Johnson Ent. Agency

For his part, Crane saw the drummer change — especially in the middle of a successful tour — as an uncomfortable shift, as he explained in *New Musical Express*: "It was difficult finding a good drummer when Carl left. We were well-booked at the time, and we just could not afford to come off the road."

Palmer would finally breathe a sigh of relief when Crane took the news of his departure exceedingly well. "Vincent took the news great, as I knew a great friend would. Me leaving Rooster was the most amicable split ever."

For the next six months, Palmer would be in constant rehearsals with ELP, while watching Atomic Rooster achieve their first hit record with 'Tomorrow Night.' He couldn't help but feel uneasy with the irony of the situation as he saw his former band score a hit with his last effort before he left, hoping for greener pastures.

"I felt like I had made a terrible mistake leaving Atomic Rooster. 'Tomorrow Night' was a big hit six months later, and I was still rehearsing with ELP, while my old band had just had their first hit.

"I thought I had just shot myself in the foot."

8
Bring On The Hit

Atomic Rooster emerged from Palmer's departure as a much stronger band. Still a trio, with Du Cann and Hammond joining, the band now had a heavier, darker sound that aligned perfectly with Crane's brooding, intense, and often mentally unstable lyrical themes.

With Palmer gone, it was clear that Crane became the de facto leader and musical guide for the band, and this shift also gave full reign to his mental disorders, which could surface at any given moment.

Du Cann and Hammond were likely too absorbed in the excitement of being part of a rock and roll band to question Crane's often erratic mental state. However, this was not the case for roadie Donal Gallagher. Gallagher, the younger brother of emerging Irish blues guitarist Rory, worked for Crane and Rooster while Rory was taking stock of his career following the break-up of his band, Taste.

Gallagher didn't shy away from commenting on Crane's mental state, and years later, he spoke candidly to *The Afterword*: "Everything was very intense after a gig. If Vince wasn't happy with how it had gone, there'd be this aura of depression hanging over the place. You'd walk in and say 'Brilliant gig, guys,' only to be met with Vince's sullen 'Yeah? You think so?'"

In truth, despite Crane's pessimism, there was a strong sense of optimism surrounding Atomic Rooster in the early seventies.

Live, the band performed with a ferocity that, in later years, would lead to comparisons with the likes of Black Sabbath, Uriah Heep, and Deep Purple. With an eye on worldwide success, the band had secured a US distribution deal with Elektra Records.

In July, they performed on the second day of the two-day Euro-Pop '70 festival at the Eissport Stadion in Munich. Although positioned low on the bill, they shared the stage with ten other bands, including Deep Purple, Traffic, Free, Van der Graaf Generator, and Savoy Brown.

The 9,000-strong crowd gave them a fantastic reception. Crane told *Beat Instrumental*, "John fell over right in the dramatic part of his solo, but he kept on playing. At that moment, everyone in the audience was on their feet. I thought it was very good planning."

The warm reception Atomic Rooster received in mainland Europe encouraged them to spend more time there, but they also had their sights set on the US. "We want to get there and have a crack after we've steamed full pelt into Europe, which will be great preparation. It's going to seem like a holiday to work hard in England after the States."

However, Crane wasn't particularly fond of multi-band festivals, whether indoors or outdoors, which had become a significant part of the music scene by 1970. "I think ninety per cent of the festival scene will die next year when the promoters get sick of losing money. It's inevitable. I went down to Bath, and the sound was terrible. You get 2,000 watts of PA and a strong wind, and it sounds like a merry-go-round, it really does. That's why indoor ones are better. I went to the back of the hall at Munich, and the sound was really quite good. But considering the hall at Bath, I was really disappointed. It should have been mind-blowing."

Atomic Rooster went into the studio in August 1970 and would emerge some weeks later with *Death Walks Behind You*, a dark, loud, angry and brooding peon to progressive rock and metal that literally had everything: the vibe, the lyrics, the individual and collective instrumentation and all points in between, roaring down the musical tracks like a runaway train.

Most of the album was made at Recorded Sound, but a few tracks had to be done at Island because a 16-track machine was required.

Crane was, given his penchant for total control, surprisingly generous, allowing Du Cann to either share or take full songwriting credit on five of the album's eight tracks.

With a US release secured for the album, Du Cann told *Beat Instrumental*, "At first, the record company wanted to release Atomic Rooster's first album in the States the same way they did in Europe. But that wasn't a good idea, because the album came out the same week Carl Palmer left to join Keith Emerson. This meant that when I joined and we went on tour, the band wasn't the same as it had been on the record. That's partly why we waited until we had a regular drummer before recording this one."

Du Cann also discussed the songwriting process shared between him and Vincent. "Once I get the first idea, the rest of the tune comes in on its own. If it doesn't, I just tape what I've got and leave it for a while. Often, I write a middle section and then discover that I already have the beginning and end on tape."

With Rooster now adding guitar to the mix, it also required changes to Crane's Hammond C3 setup to compensate for the absence of a bass guitar. Four cabinets, each with four 12-inch Texion speaker/amplifiers, were used to reproduce the usual organ sound, and American Acoustic amps were used for the bass.

Crane explained, "At almost every concert, someone offers to buy the Acoustics from us, usually for quite large sums of money. They're quite easily the best bass amps in the world; it's just a shame they're not available in this country."

"I don't use the same speakers as everyone else with a Hammond either, because I think they tend to produce a muffled sound. It stands to reason that if you rotate two sound sources, at one point in each revolution, the sound is going to be very dead. If you average that sound out over the entire revolution, it still won't be as sharp as a straight speaker. Unless, of course, you put microphones all around the cabinet, but then you lose the point of using the rotary unit in the first place. I don't use a Mellotron for the same reason. If I want an orchestra, I'll hire one – not use a copy like the Mellotron. They're fine if you need to transport your own backing from gig to gig, but not for anything more critical."

Crane and Du Cann had spoken to *Beat Instrumental* in the upmarket Knightsbridge district of London, just a couple of days before Atomic Rooster's tour of Germany, France, and Scandinavia.

Du Cann had been with Vincent for only nine months at this point but had already gained a reputation for his superb, though somewhat unorthodox, playing style. "I don't use a Wah-wah or fuzz for effects. My playing is basically speed, with a fair bit of bending. All this sustained and contrived distortion has reached the end of its life. The public would rather hear and watch music than rate a player on his ability to hold notes for a ridiculous length of time."

"The only reason I take three instruments to each gig is for sheer practicality. I have a nasty habit of breaking strings on stage, and as far as I'm concerned, there's nothing worse than having to stand around while someone changes a string. Anyway, I play the Telecaster most and keep the Gibson SG and Stratocaster in reserve. If I could find strings that didn't break every time I got excited, I wouldn't need spares. As it is, I've decided on Clifford Essex. Once, when I was playing with Andromeda and using Fender Rock and Roll strings, I broke five out of six during one solo. Usually, I can play around a broken string, but in that case, I had to abandon the guitar!"

The extreme and over-the-top sound of *Death Walks Behind You* may have been influenced by the first signs of creative jealousy between Crane and Du Cann. In a bid to out-do each other, they literally turned everything up to ten, each trying to surpass the other's licks. At the time, this was pure speculation, but the result, despite any ruffled feathers, was that *Death Walks Behind You* emerged as the definitive Atomic Rooster album.

The album was released in September 1970 to coincide with the single 'Tomorrow Night,' which began a slow but steady climb on the UK charts. The single would remain on the charts for 12 weeks, eventually peaking at UK No. 11. By the time everything settled, *Death Walks Behind You* had reached No. 12 on the UK charts. As a debut US release, it also achieved a respectable Billboard album position at No.90.

US trade magazine *Cash Box* said of the album: "Atomic Rooster is three explosive talents from Britain: Vincent Crane (by way of Crazy World of Arthur Brown), John Cann, and Paul Hammond. The group's sound is instantly identifiable, mainly due to Crane's superlative organ and piano work. But it's also the duets Crane and Cann (electric guitar) get into, that sets this group apart. The music's texturally heavy, but the trio uses that heaviness with deft grace and aplomb. Instant success for: 'Tomorrow Night,' 'Sleeping For Years,' 'Seven Streets,' and, of course, the towering title cut."

58

9
Trouble in Rooster Land

By the final quarter of 1970, Atomic Rooster were on the verge of breaking big. However, in early 1971, rumours circulated that Elektra Records in the United States had paid a £60,000 advance for the band, as reported in the 6th February issue *Cash Box*. These rumours were swiftly denied by Elektra president Jac Holzman, who responded, "A tenth of that figure is closer to the truth."

At the same time, the first real signs of tension between Crane and Du Cann began to surface, manifesting in a fit of ego that ultimately led to much worse.

Crane also made a disparaging comment about very young fans, which prompted Erica Carter to write to *Melody Maker* in April '71:

"Please could you stop labelling everybody under 16 as a teenybopper I am thirteen and I am constantly being accused, on radio and in various musical papers of having no understanding of progressive music."

"In MM, March 27, Richard Williams found himself 'somewhat aghast that 13-year-olds could cope with Van der Graaf Generator.'"

"Also, in a recent radio interview Vincent Crane of Atomic Rooster implied that everyone under 18 was incapable of understanding heavy music — according to him we 'just applaud when everyone else does, without knowing what we're applauding about.'"

"Can't you accept that we are simply ordinary people with

an appreciation of good music and recognise it as such?"

'Tomorrow Night', as the band's breakout hit, attracted considerable attention in the rock music press. In conversation, Crane was quick to claim credit for the song's creation, but Du Cann was equally quick to assert that it was, in fact, he who had written the song.

This would become a bone of contention, simmering and then smouldering over the following months as the band embarked on a series of major festivals and club gigs. Those familiar with the inner workings of Atomic Rooster began to notice that even their finest live performances were marked by a literal musical battle, with Crane and Du Cann each attempting to outdo the other during the set.

Roadie Gallagher, who had a front-row seat to the unfolding tension, speculated that Crane was struggling internally: "He was obviously channelling a lot of negativity. There was always the feeling that he wasn't being properly appreciated as a capable musician but rather as some kind of weirdo."

Although Gallagher offset these remarks with huge praise for his musicianship: "Vince was the proverbial mad wizard, like a character from *The Lord Of The Rings*, and the improvisations he could go into had you at the edge of your seat."

Despite the growing tensions between Crane and Du Cann, the band still managed to keep any animosity in check when it mattered. In the studio, they recorded another single, 'Devil's Answer.' The song, written by Du Cann, was dark and psychologically probing, much in the same vein as the band's previous album. Released in June 1971, it had reached No. 4 on the UK charts by July 1971.

While the UK rock press hailed it as the band's major commercial breakthrough, Crane was far from ecstatic about the praise for 'Devil's Answer.'

Discussing the seeming milestone of a second hit single, Crane was pragmatic in his conversation with *New Musical Express*. "Once you've released a successful single, you've just got to do it again, otherwise you get labelled a flash-in-the-pan, one-hit wonder. You can't guarantee a hit single. It's basically just a question of luck."

Du Cann was keen to continue the dark musical vibe of *Death Walks Behind You*, while Crane, perhaps unbeknownst to Du Cann and Hammond, had decided on a funkier, more soulful direction.

The tracks for the band's next album, *In Hearing Of Atomic Rooster*, were recorded, reportedly without incident. It was at this point that Crane decided to pull the plug on Du Cann, as chronicled in *Record Collector Magazine* and *The Afterword*.

The dismissal, however, did not happen all at once.

Crane made it clear to Du Cann that he was not the ideal singer for Atomic Rooster's new direction. He was searching for a more traditional frontman who could connect with the audience, particularly with the band's shift towards a more soulful sound. Crane would eventually find his singer in Peter French, who had just come off an ill-fated stint with the band Leaf Hound and, in both appearance and vocal style, was the epitome of the rock singer.

Years later, French reflected on the experience in *Perfect Sound Forever*. He recalled, "I was asked by Vincent to join Atomic Rooster. Vincent was a superb musician and a very original composer. But I had also heard from several people about his depressive, dark nature."

Having been around the rock and roll scene long enough, French wasn't easily surprised. However, he admitted that he was a bit taken aback when, after receiving a phone call from the band's management inviting him to the studio to listen to tracks from *In Hearing of Atomic Rooster*, he found himself alone with Crane after meeting Du Cann and Hammond, as he later recalled in *The Afterword*:

"It was the most bizarre situation to walk into. All the tracks for the album had been laid down and I realised that Vincent was taking out John Du Cann's vocals and had rubbed out a lot of his guitar playing. It did seem evident that there was a contest of wills between keyboard and guitar going on. Vincent felt there was too much guitar and he wanted a proper singer who could project."

The courtship of French progressed alongside the gradual

but inevitable end of the relationship with Du Cann.

After completing the basic tracks for *In Hearing Of Atomic Rooster*, a listening session was held with Du Cann, Hammond, and record company executives. According to reports that later surfaced in *Record Collector Magazine*, Du Cann was shocked to discover that his guitar parts had been significantly reduced in the final mix, with Crane effectively burying them. Enraged by this, Du Cann reportedly smashed the offending demo vinyl to pieces before storming out.

French, though uneasy, found himself fitting in amid the disintegration of this version of Atomic Rooster. In truth, Du Cann didn't take being dismissed by Crane well at all. However, in the aftermath of his departure, Crane was surprisingly even-handed when explaining his decision in *The Afterword*:

"I knew there was a risk that if I asked John to leave, Paul would go with him because of their friendship. But I thought it was necessary to take that risk. If John stayed, I couldn't do what I wanted with the band. I would never get rid of anyone for personal reasons. The issue was with the music, and that's why John had to go."

It came as no surprise that when Du Cann and Hammond left Atomic Rooster together, in both a collective huff and a sign of their friendship, they would remain creative collaborators in whatever came next.

Du Cann and Hammond wasted no time in forming a new band, recruiting Liverpudlian vocalist Harry 'Al' Shaw and bassist/vocalist John Gustafson. Gustafson had previously been in two Liverpool bands during the 1960s, The Big Three and The Merseybeats, but teamed up with the former Rooster members following the collapse of his previous band, Quatermass.

They called themselves Bullet and quickly signed to Deep Purple's newly formed label in late 1971. Their single 'Hobo', a Du Cann composition, was the label's first 45rpm release on 19th November. The B-side, 'Sinister Minister', was credited to John Gustafson.

However, Shaw soon left the band, and they barely had time to get started before an American band with the same name threatened legal action. The trio quickly rebranded as Hard Stuff and went on to release two strong albums on the Purple label. The first, aptly titled *Bulletproof*, was followed by *Bolex Dementia*. The latter was also released in the States on Mercury, but Hard Stuff's career was ultimately short-lived.

As a final bit of trivia: a photo of the band, while still a four-piece, was used on the cover of the album *Funky Junction Play A Tribute To Deep Purple*, released in 1973. Funky Junction was essentially Thin Lizzy with additional players, and the album featured a mix of Deep Purple songs and new compositions by Leo Muller, the project's mastermind.

For the record, the ever-hustling Du Cann was noted in 1974 as the guitarist who temporarily filled in for Thin Lizzy during their tour of Germany.

With Du Cann and Hammond gone, the question arose of whether French, who had been indirectly approached about joining them in a proposed new project, would follow suit. Everyone held their breath... Until the singer made it clear that he would stick with Crane.

During this unsettled period within the band, Crane stepped away to contribute piano tracks to guitarist Rory Gallagher's self-titled debut album, on the songs 'Wave Myself Goodbye' and 'I'm Not Surprised.' Surprisingly, Crane adapted well to the role of a hired hand on the project. According to those who witnessed him during the sessions, he was the consummate professional.

10
Time Is Tight

By mid-1971, the equation was straightforward. Atomic Rooster had their best-received album to date. Andrew Bailey, writing for the *Evening Standard*, stated: "For a heavy rock outfit, Atomic performs quite tastefully. And even more importantly, it has developed a distinctive rhythmic approach. The group uses minimal distortion, managing to sound loud but pleasant. Each track has individual character, and Vincent Crane's organ is quite enterprising."

There was a hit single to help prime the international radio pump, a promising association with Elektra Records in the US, and, perhaps most importantly, an upcoming first American tour in a matter of weeks. There was just one problem.

As Bailey noted in the conclusion of his review: "A pity that the group has recently altered its line-up, making this clearly produced album a piece of history rather than an example of the group's growing prowess."

Elsewhere, *Esher News and Mail* commented: "'Total excitement' is how Vincent Crane, organist/pianist, sums up the group's music. Fair enough. If by this he means a climactic excitement, a dynamic blend of light and shade, but not, as is too often the case with their new album *In Hearing Of Atomic Rooster*, a boring reiteration of a single idea."

"Now, don't get me wrong. I'm not criticising this album as being bad. At times it's good, and at others very good, but several of the tracks are overlong, and one grows tired of a novelty through overstatement."

FRIARS Presents a Rock explosion
ATOMIC ROOSTER
COCHISE
MONDAY NOV.8. 7·45
SOUTHAMPTON GUILDHALL
ALL TICKETS 65p from the information bureau, the Junction,
Southampton. Tel: 21106. or on the night.

"One's palate can become jaded by too much of a good thing, just as easily as one can dismiss the banal and trite. Without a doubt, the group is one of the most musical around, and their songs — one hesitates to use this word, as the pieces are more an outcry against the frustrations of society than traditional lyrics — are important."

"Pete French seems to be a dynamic Dylan, shouting his fears to the world. 'Break-Through,' for example, is a superb depiction of disillusionment. 'The Price' and 'Decision/Indecision' also have very salient points to make. But, funnily enough, my two favourite tracks were the instrumentals 'The Rock' and 'Spoonful.'"

"Mind you, I must wonder why they bothered to recruit a session brass section to help things along in 'The Rock.' Their presence might have been felt, but was hardly heard, and I'm sure a few hearty organ chords would have made the same impact. Otherwise, this track features some restrained and stylish drumming from Paul Hammond, and some very nice organ from Vincent. A bouquet, too, to Roger Dean for his beautifully drawn cover. On the new Pegasus label, the Rooster bears the number Peg 1."

That new label was a subsidiary of B & C, but no sooner had *In Hearing Of Atomic Rooster* been released than Robert Masters, the group's personal manager, was discussing a new label to be launched by the Gaff Masters Co. in the New Year. By October, a pressing and distribution deal was in progress, and Masters considered the group's contract with B & C Records to be terminated.

From a purely economic standpoint, a US tour was essential at a time when Atomic Rooster had, up until that point, cultivated a profitable international audience that kept the band constantly on the road, performing to packed houses. However, Crane insisted — often amid bouts of depression and a belief that only he knew what was best for the band — that the opportunity to tour the US, opening for acts such as Alice Cooper, Cactus, Savoy Brown, Yes, and Long John Baldry, would outweigh the fact that a first US tour would most certainly operate at a loss and take the band away from their profitable touring months of August and September in Europe.

In the end, Crane's determination prevailed.

"Several people had said it was a bad time to leave England," Crane explained in an interview with *New Musical Express*. "But I've waited two years for this tour, and it wasn't going to be put off."

Crane was diligent in assembling what would be the latest line-up for the tour. He called drummer Ric Parnell, who had ironically been dismissed from Atomic Rooster a few months earlier. Like most musicians at the time, Parnell needed the money and didn't hesitate to return to the band. He knew the Rooster repertoire, was reliable in a live setting, and, truth be told, was eager for the payday that a US tour would undoubtedly bring. So, any past grievances were forgiven or forgotten, and Parnell rejoined the fold.

Parnell's father was top drummer and arranger Jack. Ric freely admitted that he didn't have the same level of technique as his father, such as paradiddles, but he had the necessary feel for the drums. He told Derek Abrahams, writing for *Beat Instrumental*, "My father was voted best drummer in England seven times but I'm nothing like him. He's given me all the encouragement I ever needed but he didn't actually teach me."

"I learned to play rhythms by tapping my hands and feet and just progressed from there. I don't think I'm a bad drummer now."

Parnell had formed his own band called Ric Parnell's Independence aged just seventeen. Realising that he wasn't cut out to be a singer he took to the drums.

He then spoke of top drummers. He started and didn't really finish, saying that it would take hours to list all of them all.

On the break-up of Independence, he got a job at NEMS and composer Tim Rice got him a gig in Cornwall with a group called Mixed Bag. Parnell said he got kicked out of the band after just three days. "They were a straight pop band and I was going into the underground scene. I don't think the two combined very well."

"After that, I had a string of different jobs. Then one

day my old man asked me if I wanted to play with Engelbert Humperdinck. I thought he was joking but discovered he wasn't when he told me the salary was £100 a week. The job meant that I had to go to America for three months, then on to Bermuda, a few appearances in Australia, Japan, and then back home."

"I didn't really fancy going around the world. I thought that I'd go to America and save plenty of money and come back to do what I wanted. I got kicked out of Humperdinck's group."

It was after this that Parnell auditioned successfully for Atomic Rooster.

That left only a guitarist and the role was quickly filled by a new kid on the UK music scene Steve Bolton who, in a phone conversation with the author, recalled how it all came to be.

"A few months after I arrived in London, I was playing guitar during midnight shows at a London strip club, when I happened to see an advert in *Melody Maker* 'Atomic Rooster requires lead guitarist for American tour to start immediately.' I answered the ad. I wasn't really a lead guitar player, but I managed to book an audition in two days' time. In those two days, I desperately taught myself lead guitar licks. I auditioned, went back to my gig at the strip club. Then I got a call. I got the gig."

A quick week's rehearsal and a couple of warm-up gigs and the latest line-up of Atomic Rooster was primed and road-ready for their assault on America. For Bolton, in conversation with the author, it was a mind-bending experience for the still-wet-behind-the-ears youngster.

"It was my first big tour with a name band. It was an amazing experience for me. The fans were great, the women were all over the place. The band was going down really well. It was just an amazing experience."

In later years, French, in an *Afterword* and *Furious.com* excerpt, was equally enthralled with his first up-close and personal look at the rock life on a massive level. "For me, it was like a driving a high-speed motorcar for the first time. I liked the way that American audiences went all out to enjoy

Friars Earth Enterprises and
Gaff Masters Ltd. present
Atomic
Rooster
in Concert
(Final dates before U.S. Tour)
Special Guests
NAZARETH
Wednesday, 3rd November:
Cith Hall, Newcastle-upon-Tyne.
Sunday, 7th November:
Guild Hall, Plymouth
Monday, 8th November:
Guild Hall, Southampton
Thursday, 11th November:
Town Hall, Middlesbrough
Saturday, 13th November:
Glyderdrome, Boston
Sunday, 14th November:
Kings Hall, Derby.

themselves."

Although Bolton and French recall the US tour fondly, the review of the gig at the Hara Arena in Dayton, Ohio, provides insight into why it became Atomic Rooster's one and only venture across the pond.

Atomic Rooster were third on the bill, following Cactus and headliners Alice Cooper. Tom Scheidt, writing for the *Journal Herald*, pulled no punches in his review: "The near capacity house was first entertained by Atomic Rooster. Boredom set in almost immediately as each song sounded like the previous one — dull and unoriginal."

"Lead singer, Peter French was a poor Mick Jagger. His voice was unimpressive when it could be heard. The organist needed polish, the drummer was too loud and the lead guitarist created a muddy sound. The talking between songs was absolutely pointless. The Rooster was less than atomic."

Indeed, John Mendelsohn's review for the *Los Angeles Times* of Atomic Rooster's appearance at the Whisky in LA in December was equally as critical, particularly singling out Peter French: "England's Atomic Rooster, on display at The Whisky, through the weekend, recalls the least attractive features of Emerson Lake & Palmer and Black Sabbath. Its music is leaden and plodding, flashy but without much real substance, and depends to an inordinate extent on unusually timed interchanges between organ and rhythm section to dispel the monotony."

"The spoilt presence in the group of an obnoxious lead singer whose surly pose-ridden manner suggests a number of the late Jim Morrison's lesser imitators and whose vocals are abrasive without being even minimally soulful helps Rooster matters not a trifle."

"Group boss Vincent Crane went through several sets of sidemen before achieving (inexplicable) satisfaction with the current line-up and format. His energies would have been more wisely expended learning to live with Arthur Brown, for the success of whose legendary Crazy World he was perhaps as much as 50% responsible."

Concerning the concert at the Municipal Auditorium

Hard Stuff: solid boogie style . . .

JOHN CANN is a guitar player who's always had this thing in his head about playing heavy music, but heavy music good and true.

That's why nearly a year ago he split from what he reckoned was a badly ailing Atomic Rooster to attempt getting an outfit together which would be more sympathetic to his approach to playing rock and roll. Drummer Paul Hammond also left Rooster, apparently for much the same reasons, to join up with John and John Gustafson, the veteran bass player from the early sixties Liverpool scene and several more recent bands, came in to complete a trio which took to the road during the latter half of last year under the name Bullett.

Since then they've been obliged to change their name to avoid confusion for it was just their luck that another Bullett, an American band found themselves with a freak hit on their hands in Britain, so Cann's Bullett switched their name to a fairly apt but unsubtle Hard Stuff.

When they were known as Bullett, the band got off to an encouraging start when last November they supported Deep Purple during their British tour which, says Cann, helped gell the band far quicker than had they stuck to the normal club and college scene and they were given a second booster at the beginning of this year when they supported the amazingly popular Uriah Heep on their British tour.

Hard Stuff's recently released debut album, out on Purple Records, reveals that the group are in fact getting near to what Cann says he's aiming for — a kind of solid boogie with a lot of musical value. Cann lists Jeff Beck as being one of his main influences. He's never been a Clapton freak, although he digs a few blues players like Buddy Guy.

Along with John Gustafson, John writes most of the band's material, some of which he wrote while in Atomic Rooster but for some reason or other turned out to be unsuitable for inclusion in Rooster's repertoire. That's only one of the many grouses John Cann voices against his old band.

"Rooster was too insipid at times," said John. "Too much organ with no bass just didn't sound good and there never seemed to be any balls in the music. We tried telling Vincent (Crane) to get a bass guitarist in but he'd never listen."

The next Hard Stuff album is already nearly completed but it probably won't be released until the Autumn. John's confident that it'll do well.

"The album we have out just now is selling pretty well, despite some knocks we've been getting from the press. It's the same with our live gigs, the audiences really dig it but then the press will give us a poor review. I think that's kinda strange."

There are a lot of bands jostling each other for favour on the British heavy rock scene these days. Black Sabbath, Uriah Heep and Deep Purple are the big daddies on this particular wicket — whether there's room for one more only time will tell. — RAY TELFORD with Savoy Brown, Bob Denham for the *San Antonio Express and News* was a bit more forgiving and acknowledged that "in all fairness it must be said the scurrying in the background by the stage crew may have been due to mixing problems which led to the bad effect."

Having used the same cliché to say that they put on a performance that was less than atomic, Denham said, "The best that can be said is that they held nothing back. In fact, that was the problem. Every song was played practically one-way, full blast. Instead of a group paying together, it almost was as if they were trying to outdo one another."

Although Denham concluded by saying their last number, 'Gershatzer,' "written and played by Vincent Crane was well worth the wait through the rest of the performance."

To give balance, Celeste Carlisle for the *Deseret News* was positive about the band's performance at the British all-day gig at the Coliseum in Salt Lake City. Originally scheduled for the Speedway track, the gig had to be switched to the indoor venue because of heavy rain.

Adding to the woes, Atomic Rooster, who were second on the bill to Savoy Brown, were late, delayed for hours in Idaho. As Carlisle said, "Their enthusiasm flowed into tired, music-saturated kids. For many the concert had started ten hours ago."

"Rooster played a tight, energy-charged set and returned eagerly for an encore, which is rare among rock groups. There were barely enough people present at the end to raise sound for an encore, yet Atomic Rooster members jumped back on stage."

Record World had reported in September that *Death Walks Behind You*, already out of date in terms of line-up, was hot on the charts, racking up strong album sales in the course of their thirty-city tour American tour — according to Elektra's Vice-president of sales Mel Posner, but Atomic Rooster didn't land on American soil again.

11
Crash And Burn

The relationship between Crane and French initially seemed promising, particularly in the live setting of the US tour. The line-up was starting to gel, and Atomic Rooster continued to be a powerful force on stage.

Crane's vision for the band — stripped back to the essential elements of prog rock, with none of the unnecessary baggage — was being well received by American audiences, despite occasional lukewarm reviews from the press. Behind the scenes, however, the internal chemistry within the group was growing increasingly fragile. Just two months into the tour, tensions were rising.

Reflecting on the period, French addressed these issues candidly in interviews with *Get Ready To Rock* and *The Vinyl Press*:

"Vincent was a great musician to perform with, but what I was missing was that good old rock guitar sound. Vincent was also proving to be a difficult man to communicate with. His depression was getting worse. There wasn't the freedom within the band to put my stamp or influence on the writing that I had hoped for. Although I gained plenty of experience from the performances, I gained very little else — and we were making hardly any money." (Reportedly £60 a week.)

During the US tour, Atomic Rooster shared bills with the American heavy rock and blues band Cactus, whose members Tim Bogart and Carmine Appice were so impressed by French's stage presence that they approached him with an offer to join their band.

"It was while I was touring the States with Atomic Rooster that Tim Bogart and Carmine Appice came to me and said they wanted me to leave Atomic Rooster and front Cactus," French recalled in interviews with *The Sledgelord.com*, *Furious.com*, and others.

Though flattered, French found himself caught in a difficult position. Despite the rough patches, he still felt a sense of loyalty to the band that had, up to that point, given him his first big break.

A mid-tour break brought Atomic Rooster back to the UK, where they secured a coveted slot as the opening act at a massive outdoor concert headlined by The Who and The Faces. For French, what happened next would prove to be the final straw.

During a heated argument between Crane and French about how the band would get to the gig, Crane exploded: "Take the bloody bus to the gig!" He said, 'Take a bus!' Not even the offer of a cab." French knew in that moment that his brief tenure with Atomic Rooster was coming to an end.

"I realised that I was not going to get any further musically," he later told *Furious.com*, "and so I decided to take the opportunity and join Cactus."

Breaking the news to Crane proved to be a moment thick with tension, as French recounted across *Furious.com*, *Steve Hoffman Music Forums.com*, and *The Afterword*:

"I told Vincent that I had, had enough and that I was going to leave and join Cactus. Vincent did not want to lose me. He said, 'Who the hell do you think you are?' He said, 'You can't go to America!' I said, 'Watch this space.'"

French was clear that it was Crane's arrogance that sealed his decision: "I told him nobody tells me what to do. So, I left."

12
Made In England...
Rest In Pieces

French was barely out the door when Crane was already once again fine-tuning Atomic Rooster.

Within weeks, he had completely turned the band on its head — shifting from a hard rock outfit with pronounced progressive leanings to a group now sounding like an amalgamation of soul and funk. It was less Atomic Rooster and more a mutation of James Brown.

This transformation led him to call up veteran soul singer Chris Farlowe — admittedly more of a pure soul and gospel vocalist than a rock frontman — who had recently found himself out of work following his stint with Colosseum. Farlowe was more than willing to join Atomic Rooster.

According to *Record Collector Magazine*, Farlowe's entry into the band was, quite literally, a cash-up-front arrangement. Crane reportedly handed him a thousand dollars in cash to seal the deal. While such a transaction might seem dubious by today's standards, at the time, money changing hands for any number of reasons was entirely de rigueur.

One person who had a ringside seat for the beginning of the Farlowe era was Derek Abrahams of *Beat Instrumental*, who provided a first-hand account of those early moments as he travelled with the band to Düsseldorf, West Germany, for their first gig with the new singer.

MARQUAY
TORQUAY TOWN
2 DAY THING HALL.
TORBAY BLUES FESTIVAL
KEEF HARTLEY BAND and OTHERS
FRI 31st JULY.
ATOMIC ROOSTER SAT 1st AUG
WISHBONE ASH
Lights by 'Speed Freak'
Carbon Dioxide Bottles
ADOLPHUS REBIRTH
of Joy.
Booze in Bar
These Bands will also be appearing. Words by Davy Jones
FREEZE
Tickets: 12/6 FRI/10/- SAT/£1 Both from :- Tangerine Fuzz, Market St Torquay Tel. 22585, John Cerways, Abbey Rd Torquay, or A.E. Orne Tobacconist. 5b. Fleet St. Torquay (opposite W.H. Smith). or at door on night.

RAINBOW PAVILION TORQUAY HARBOURSIDE
SUNDAY 30th JULY 1972
ATOMIC ROOSTER
STRIFE · DAVY JONES
Coming Sunday 6th August FAIRPORT CONVENTION
MARQUAY · TORQUAY TOWN HALL
WEDNESDAY 2nd AUG 1972
CHICKEN SHACK · BRINSLEY SCHWARTZ
LIGHTS BY MR. ZAPP · DISCO · DAVY JONES
Coming Wed 9th August STATUS QUO

ARTHUR BROWN'S
KINGDOM COME
AT RAG BALL
featuring
AT TIFFANY'S 25 MARCH

Vincent Crane was visibly anxious, pacing nervously up and down the airport lounge. His wife, Pat, struggled to keep up with him, trying to reassure him that everything would be all right. Ric Parnell, equally tense, chain-smoked and frequently adjusted the brim of his black Mafioso-style hat. Steve Bolton sat perfectly still, gazing out of the window in silence.

They were due to meet Chris Farlowe in Essen, which may have explained the collective anxiety. "Christ! I hope everything goes well," muttered Parnell.

Abrahams gathered from the band that, after some intense rehearsals, they were confident Farlowe had a good grasp of the songs. He had taken the lyrics home to learn, but there was still uncertainty as to whether he had absorbed them well enough to perform in front of an anticipated 12,000 fans.

Also at the airport were five members of Osibisa, who were also scheduled to perform at the same gig. For a brief moment, Parnell seemed to forget his nerves when he spotted Osibisa's bassist, Spartacus R (real name Roy Bedeau), wandering nearby. "I'd give anything to be able to play with Osibisa," he said. "I've been experimenting with congas and timbales. Can you imagine Rooster and Osibisa jamming together? I bet I could give a good account of myself."

Crane, having somewhat composed himself — though noticeably paler than usual — joined the rest of the group as they made their way toward the departure gate. Osibisa followed closely behind, with Parnell walking just ahead of them. Perhaps he wanted onlookers to think he was part of their entourage.

Abrahams joined the group on the flight, seated between Bolton and Parnell. Across the aisle, Crane and Pat held hands in silence.

Parnell kept up the conversation with Abrahams, sometimes veering into whimsical territory in a manner that seemed emblematic of the 1970s: "I wish I could fly without a plane. Just take off like a bird. I'll do it one day." Then, returning to earth, he added: "I'd love to get into studio productions and electronics. I want to use a studio the way Pink Floyd do. The effects they get are incredible, and I want the same. It'd be great to take a studio on the road with Rooster, so we could record whenever we wanted. We might do that one day."

He also spoke of his admiration for John Bonham, citing him as an influence for his taste, style, and technique. He praised Bernard Purdie, especially for his work with King Curtis, and described Buddy Rich as "probably the greatest all-round drummer in the world. It's even more unbelievable that he was already the greatest when my old man was my age."

Upon landing in Düsseldorf, Parnell was stopped and questioned by customs. As they searched his bag, they found some cone-shaped tablets, which he managed to explain were incense. The officer continued rummaging and pulled out a rubber chicken. He stared at Parnell as if he were mad. The explanation — that he throws the rooster into the audience at the end of shows — was met with a typically blank, bureaucratic expression before the item was returned and he was waved through.

Crane and his wife Pat also received the full German security treatment, being semi-stripped and searched. Eventually, however, everyone cleared customs, where they were met by the band's manager, Robert Masters, who ushered them into waiting cars and off to their hotel — the Hotel Arnold, in nearby Essen.

Before long, Chris Farlowe arrived to join the group. He promptly sat down with Crane to discuss in detail the songs he had learned and how he planned to approach them.

Chris Farlowe's debut gig with Atomic Rooster took place at the Grugahalle in Essen, as part of an event billed as the Essen-Pop Carnival. Kicking off at 4:00pm on Saturday 12th February, the multi-band concert was quite the spectacle, running non-stop until 6:30 on Sunday morning. Alongside the musical performances, the event also featured a screening of *The Beatles' Yellow Submarine*, as well as knife-throwers, magicians, and high-wire artists.

The audience certainly got their money's worth. In addition to these attractions, the musical line-up was extensive and impressive, featuring: Linda Lewis, Curtis & Maldoon, Principal Edwards Magic Theatre, Tucky Buzzard, Pretty Things, Beggars

Opera, Palladin, Atomic Rooster, Osibisa, and Deep Purple.

Prior to the performance, Vincent Crane spoke with Derek Abrahams about his early years, including his time studying at Trinity College, and praised his brilliant tutor. "There was a lot of training. Part of it meant I had to write a piece of classical music for the tutor. I usually only managed to write half of it, and he astonished me regularly by guessing how the rest went. Another part of the course called for orchestral improvisation, which was also really difficult."

"I'd have liked to go into classical music full-time, but I think eighteen is too late to start thinking about it. While I was at Trinity, I also played with a jazz trio at the Marquee."

Crane also reflected on former singer Pete French, who had often complained about being unable to hear himself over the instrumentation. "We used to have to write down the structure of a certain melody line that was played to us. We also had to decipher a four-part harmony being played on the piano. It's really difficult when there's an orchestral instrument involved. I know all that training has helped me a lot, because now I can hear everything the rest of the group are playing. I can also hear what the singer is singing."

On the subject of replacing John Du Cann, Crane explained that Steve Bolton had joined the band after a long and exhaustive audition process.

"There were about eighty guitarists, I think," Crane recalled. "After a while I just couldn't distinguish one from the other. But Steve was the best, so he came with us. Then came Ric. He joined after another audition we held. We were really worried about the drumming side of things because we wanted a funky drummer, but just couldn't seem to find one. Ric was the only reasonably funky drummer who turned up. He's improved a lot since."

Back to the gig, and Farlowe had run through last-minute rehearsals in the dressing room, covering 'Tomorrow Night,' 'Breakthrough,' 'Save Me,' 'A Spoonful Of Bromide Helps The Pulse Rate Go Down,' 'Decision/Indecision,' 'The Price,' 'Gershatzer,' and 'Devil's Answer.'

Farlowe was already immensely popular in Germany

Farlowe joins Rooster

CHRIS FARLOWE, former Colosseum vocalist joined Atomic Rooster at the weekend, and Pete French has left the band to work in America. The new line up consists of Vincent Crane (organ), Chris Farlowe (vocals), Steve Bolton (lead guitar) and Rick Parnell (drums) and the group will start work almost immediately. From February 11-20 they tour Germany, and on February 24 they make their debut in this country at the Memorial Hall, Barry.

Commenting on the move, Chris Farlowe told SOUNDS this week: "I'm looking forward to singing much more funky music, which is more my bag".

Said Vincent: "Chris was a natural choice for the band and I feel that this new combination is something I have been working for for a long time."

following his stint with Colosseum, and thousands in the audience rose to their feet upon his announcement. As Abrahams observed, "When he appeared, it was as though Moses had returned from the peak of a mountain with the tablets of stone in his hands."

He added, "The gig was superb. Perhaps a little theatrical, with Crane falling supposedly senseless to the floor after a long keyboard solo. Bolton jumped in the air at certain moments, and Parnell did his moody and savage piece when the time was right. Generally, however, their performance was spontaneous and the audience loved every minute of it."

"Deep Purple had a difficult time following them — I wasn't the only one to say so, either."

"The PA, which had gone wrong earlier, sounded as though it was breaking up a bit during some numbers, but generally it held together. Crane's organ had been wired up incorrectly — the keyboard somehow managed to produce different volumes from the pedals — but he managed to cope."

"Considering it was the group's first gig with Farlowe, they all looked thoroughly pleased with themselves when their set was through. Farlowe said he had to guess a couple of times whether he was singing the right tune and whether it was the right moment to come in. Crane said he could hear everything."

After the gig, Crane remarked, "On-stage professionalism is what makes a band. They are there to play, and they must play as best as they can. The audience don't care if the band isn't feeling in the mood. They've paid money — sometimes a lot of money — and they have every right to demand perfection. I think they got it with Rooster tonight."

After their performance, the band stayed to watch Deep Purple before returning to the hotel to continue the discussion.

Years later, Farlowe would acknowledge in a podcast interview hosted by keyboard player Rick Wakeman that he was not overly enthusiastic at the prospect. "I was out of work and needed the money, so I agreed. What they were doing was not really my kind of music, but I figured that I would stick it out for a year."

Farlowe also had interests outside of music. His shop,

Call To Arms, located on Islington's Upper Street in London, specialised in military memorabilia, including German paraphernalia. However, Farlowe was quick to emphasise that he was deeply patriotic, stating he would be the first to sign up if Britain's shores were ever threatened.

To Farlowe, Call To Arms was a sideline — a space where he could reflect on his main profession in the music world. "The shop is a total escape for me from show business," he told *Beat Instrumental* in early 1973.

"During my Colosseum days, Jon Hiseman told me that he lived the band twenty-four hours a day because he had nothing else to focus on. He said he envied me because I had other activities to channel my thoughts into."

During the interview, conducted over coffee and sandwiches in a small café around the corner from his shop, Farlowe showed off a ring he was wearing. It was silver and bore the Swastika. "She gave it to me," he said, nodding towards the woman behind the café counter. "She's Italian but won't tell me where she got it from. Will you?"

He shouted the last two words so she could hear him. She instantly understood what he was referring to but simply laughed and repeated what she'd told him many times before.

"She probably knew a German during the war but won't say," he said, then added with a theatrical bellow worthy of any Teutonic general, "If you won't tell me where you got it from, give me a buttered bun instead."

****

With Bolton and Parnell somewhat bemused but ultimately willing to embrace this new musical direction — despite growing grumbles from those aware of the stylistic shift — this incarnation of Atomic Rooster played a series of warm-up gigs before heading into Trident Studios to record *Made In England* in a lightning-fast session.

Despite Crane's increasing insistence on doing things his way, *Made In England* was notable for his willingness to share songwriting credits with Bolton and Parnell. Bolton would later admit that, at the time, his songwriting skills were virtually non-existent, and that he was learning on the job, as he explained in conversation with the author.

"I was young and just happy to be playing in a top band," Bolton recalled. "The band was really funky in those sessions, and my experience as a rhythm player really helped. I had never written a song in my life, so I just wrote them — 'Never To Lose' and 'Space Cowboy'. I really can't remember how it happened. I just put the songs to the band and they recorded them."

The band were scheduled to appear at the Reading Festival in August, but in his article for the *Reading Evening Post* on 7th July, Pete Butterfield jumped the gun slightly in his feature on the new line-up. He wrote: "...the line-up is completed by the distinctive voice of Chris Farlowe. Next month will see a return to Reading of one of Britain's most powerful rock singers. He was at last year's festival with Colosseum. Perhaps this year Chris and his band will come to the fore, although he is rumoured to have some stiff opposition — notably from Rod Stewart and The Faces."

Alas, Atomic Rooster never even made it to the perimeter fence.

However, Butterfield did manage to provide a preview of the forthcoming album: "This album, their first for their new label, is a belter with a great depth of feeling. The production seems a trifle muddy here and there, but it doesn't detract — in fact, it makes it sound all the more authentic and true to their live sound."

"They don't carry a bassman, and Crane puts the bass part in on organ or electric piano. This is what he has done on the album, apart from one track, and I think this accounts for the rather boomy feel."

"My favourites from the album are the two opening tracks, 'Time Take My Life' and 'Stand By Me,' the latter being the band's latest single. They both drive along with force, Farlowe singing in pedigree Rooster fashion — in fact, the ex-Thunderbird is flying to new heights."

"Crane is, of course, the shining light. His compositions are beautifully constructed with good, funky rhythms — and

Open air Concert
HARROW, SATURDAY, JULY 15
John Peel introduces
Stone the Crows
Smith Perkins Smith
Atomic Rooster
Patto : Walrus
MUSIC
STARTS
11 a.m.
at
Wealdstone Football Club
Station Road, Harrow, Middx.
Tickets from: Keith Prowse & Agents
£1 Advance : £1.25 at the gate
Tube: Harrow on the Hill, Harrow &
Wealdstone
Buses. 140, 114, 183, 158, 182, 186,
286

SAT 22nd JULY
Gaff Masters ltd. In association with
The Nottingham Festival, presents....
GOOSE FAIR
FOREST RECREATION GROUND,
NOTTINGHAM
NAZARETH
BYZANTIUM
FACES
ASHMAN
REYNOLDS
ATOMIC ROOSTER - STATUS QUO
MARMALADE Plus support groups
BILL SUBJECT TO ALTERATION
Advance tickets £1.50 each
Tickets on the day if available £2.00
Tickets from:
Festival Booking
Office,
Old Market Square,
Nottingham.
Gaff Masters Ltd.,
90 Wardour St.,
London W1.
Barker & Co.,
91 The Headrow,
Leeds 1.
Wilson Peck,
64-70 Leopold St.,
Sheffield.
Hine and Addison,
37 John Dalton St.,
Manchester 1.

his jazz piano or organ stamps an indelible character on all the songs. Steve Bolton and Ric Parnell also contribute with songs, but it's Crane who comes over as the maestro."

"One fault with the album — and it has nothing to do with the music. Some bright spark decided to make the cover out of denim. It's great for patching your jeans, but a devil to file in a record collection."

The *Evening Despatch*, a newspaper based in England's Northeast, wrote: "They are at their best when they let rip on powerhouse numbers like 'Stand By Me,' with the band roaring away behind Chris Farlowe's shouting vocals. Chris really comes across as a singer of many moods on this LP: breathless on 'Never Lose,' shrill and high-pitched on 'Close Your Eyes,' and demonstrating great control and power across all the tracks."

"Vincent Crane, on organ and electric piano, is the inspiration behind the group, laying down some heavy bass lines on the more rocking numbers."

"His experiments with the ARP synthesiser, however, are a waste of time, and 'All In Satan's Name' shows how not to use electronics for effect."

"Atomic Rooster remind me of an R&B band in the mould of Chris Farlowe and The Thunderbirds — but brought up to date."

Made In England was released in July 1972, and it immediately sparked division among critics and long-time Rooster fans. Taken on its own merits, the album is a unique piece of work, blending soul, funk, gospel, and jazz elements into a series of both sonic and introspective moments. Repeated listens do not diminish the overall impression of Made In England as a largely successful creative turn for the band.

However, these positive reactions were largely overshadowed by a sense of betrayal felt by Rooster fans who had been with the band from the beginning. In short, *Made In England* was met with indifference to the band's new direction.

The glaring evidence of the album's failure came in the form of its lack of commercial success. Both *Made In England*

and its single, 'Stand By Me,' failed to chart in the UK, which had always been considered the band's stronghold. Internationally, the album fared little better. In the US, the album peaked at No. 149 on the charts, while it reached No. 60 in Canada and No. 42 in Australia.

The dismal reception of *Made In England* seemed to amplify existing tensions within the band.

The band's record label, Dawn, was also growing frustrated with the album's lack of commercial appeal and was pressuring the band to produce something more marketable. Although Atomic Rooster continued to be a popular live draw — indeed, during a show in Milan, the police had to resort to using tear gas to prevent fans from storming the already packed venue. One policeman was injured and eleven fans arrested — financial issues also continued to haunt the band.

The latest casualty of this tension was Bolton, who decided to leave in search of what he felt would be a better opportunity. "I was young," Bolton told the author, "and I wanted to move on."

Crane remained determined that Atomic Rooster should continue, and he quickly found a replacement in guitarist John Goodsall, who would perform under the name Johnny Mandala while with the band.

"Ric Parnell got me that job," Goodsall explained in *Music Without Borders.com*. "Bolton was leaving, and Ric and I were determined to play together. I was in Atomic Rooster for four years, and we toured Europe constantly. It was all pretty wild — we were young and reckless. If I had known better, I would have nurtured the situation for much longer."

Meanwhile, Farlowe was enjoying himself and relishing the break from Atomic Rooster. With a big tour coming up, he told *Beat Instrumental* in early '73 that he had just finished recording his first solo album "with a few friends," which was reportedly due for release around that time.

"I work regularly for a while, then take a break. Usually, I get some songs written, then go back into the studio to sing them. The group's got a new lead guitarist now, and we're all getting it together with him."

Although the album never materialised, Farlowe was advertised to perform at the Lanchester Arts Festival in Coventry on 4th February. The line-up was set to include Rick Wakeman, Tony Iommi of Black Sabbath, Keith Moon, and notably, former Atomic Rooster drummer Carl Palmer, as well as a host of other big-name stars.

However, the event turned into a fiasco, with hundreds of ticket-holders demanding refunds when only Keith Moon and former Bonzo Dog Doo-Dah Band member Vivian Stanshall appeared. Reading between the lines, it seemed the organisers had announced several musicians before any confirmations or agreements had taken place.

****

Crane was determined that the attitude behind *Made In England* had potential, so he wasted little time getting the once again reconfigured Atomic Rooster line-up into the studio to record *Nice 'n' Greasy*.

However, the vibe during the making of *Nice 'n' Greasy* was somewhat strained. The rift between Dawn Records and Crane was deepening, resulting in an attitude of simply getting something out there rather than focusing on creating a good album. Once again, Atomic Rooster embraced a soul/funk vibe. To a large extent, *Nice 'n' Greasy* was a jam album, with the most notable aspect being the obvious remake of the band's classic track 'Friday The 13th,' reworked as 'Save Me.'

For his part, Mandala was a staunch supporter of the session and the album. "*Nice 'n' Greasy* was a very interesting record to make, and it still sounds good today. It really sounds like us."

However, *Nice 'n' Greasy* would go down in the eyes of both critics and fans as the worst Atomic Rooster album to date, reportedly selling only 500 copies by the time the dust settled.

Douglas Goodlad summed it up in his *Time Off* column for the *Leicester Chronicle*: "*Nice 'n' Greasy* features one of my favourite singers, Chris Farlowe, who has recently departed from the band. I can see why after hearing this album. The material is very samey and mediocre, and there's an air of disinterest throughout the album — almost as though the group were compelled to produce an LP without ideas. The only thing I liked about it was the cover showing a fag end stubbed into a day-old fried egg. A really fine no-smoking ad."

There was no charting single, and the album itself failed to make an impact on the charts. In response to the critical and commercial failure, Dawn Records dropped Atomic Rooster from the label. At this point, that particular line-up of the band effectively ceased to exist, with Farlowe, Parnell, and Mandala leaving to pursue more lucrative opportunities, leaving Crane to fend for himself.

With European tour dates already locked in, Crane decided to finish the remaining live gigs by recruiting members of the Sam Apple Pie band to fill the vacancies, rebranding the group as Vincent Crane's Atomic Rooster.

One such gig was at Cleopatra's in Derby and reviewed by Alan Smith for the local *Evening Telegraph*: "A lone zebra pranced and danced and tossed her mane in time with the music as Atomic Rooster weaved some amazing threads of sounds into highly heady rock patterns at Cleopatra's on Thursday."

"The girl in the horizontally striped dress was the only one to brave the floor, while Rooster's music can inspire the urge to freak, it is mostly for listening."

"And unlike some of their previous visits to Derby, the sounds they generated were well worth listening to. Vincent Crane is the sole survivor of the original Atomic Rooster, and his background of playing organ with a jazz trio, is at last shining through the rock for which Rooster is famed."

"Sitting or standing behind a bank of keyboards he pushes out the sound with accomplished skill and obvious enjoyment, his long black hair swaying to the beat as he arches his back and lurches towards the black and white grinning expanses of keys, setting the whole tower of instruments rocking until they almost topple over."

"Robbo the Roadie rushes on stage to prevent the heavy block from crashing onto the amps and then some wag in the mob bawls out song lyrics above the piercing and often chunky guitar work of Geoff Dixon."

"Drummer Willa Campbell (sic) knits his cymbals neatly, providing an Inter City rapid rhythm to it, with devastating explosions to punctuate and fire the whole picture. "

"Dave Hawkmooa is a very important guy in the Rooster set-up. He's the roadie in charge of mixing. And on Thursday he did an excellent job, keeping the volume just right. None of that wall-shattering stuff that I had the misfortune to suffer at Tiffany's a couple of years back."

"Vincent told me afterwards that they had now progressed on more musical lines and were not playing so loud anymore. They have just finished a European tour and have a new album out next month. It should be well worth a spin or two."

The drummer mentioned by Smith was more than likely Wilgar Campbell, who had previously been with Rory Gallagher. Guitarist Geoff Dixon doesn't crop up anywhere else in the Atomic Rooster history and the mention of him clearly shows how unstable the performing Atomic Rooster line-ups were during this period.

During this period, Crane managed to secure a one-off deal with Decca Records to release the single 'Tell Your Story Sing Your Song' by Vincent Crane's Atomic Rooster. While the track was reasonably catchy in a pop sense, it ultimately failed to chart.

The grim state of Atomic Rooster — and particularly Crane's mindset — was best captured in the album notes Crane wrote for *Nice 'n' Greasy*. He described one track as: "This track is best heard in the family crypt at midnight while a full moon chases shadows through the tombstones."

In January 1974, the band made the press for all the wrong reasons. "Row Explodes Over Atomic Rooster" ran the headline in the *Lancashire Telegraph*.

The controversy stemmed from the last-minute cancellation of a concert at King George's Hall in Blackburn. The gig was cancelled with less than forty-eight hours' notice after Vincent Crane reportedly fell ill with hepatitis.

This sparked a row between Terry King Enterprises, the showbiz agency representing Atomic Rooster, and the social committee of Blackburn Students' Union. The committee decided that it would be unfair to the ticket holders to proceed with an alternative band.

"People have paid to see one thing, and it wouldn't be fair for them to turn up and see someone else," said social secretary David Evans.

However, with Rooster's no-show, the supporting act — Darryl Way's Wolf — threatened to sue the committee over the cancellation.

"I don't know if there will be a concert with the same group on another date," Evans said. "There is a lot of bad feeling between ourselves and the agency over this."

More than £30 worth of tickets had already been sold, and organisers were expecting between 700 and 1,000 attendees.

Ted Lemon, the public relations officer for Terry King Enterprises, stated, "Vincent Crane is the backbone of the band, and obviously we couldn't continue without him. Just this one concert and recording sessions have been called off for now. Atomic Rooster may have to cancel two or three other concerts next week if he hasn't recovered."

The last official Atomic Rooster gig would take place in February 1975, after which Crane had, had enough and retired the band name.

Crane figuratively slipped off into the night.

13
Where Roosters Go: The Early Seventies

By the time Atomic Rooster's seemingly final incarnation disbanded, most of the musicians who had helped the band make its mark had long since moved on to other projects.

Given how badly the band had seemingly fallen from grace, the musicians of Atomic Rooster were often unfairly dismissed as faceless journeymen — young, varying in experience, and ready to jump at the first sign of something more lucrative, creative, or exciting.

It seemed that Crane, for better or worse, took these sensibilities into account when assembling the band's various line-ups. It always boiled down to a give-and-take chemistry, with both sides contributing and compromising.

In hindsight, Pete French's decision to leave Atomic Rooster for Cactus may have been a misstep. At the time, Cactus was experiencing its own disarray, with line-up changes and some internal squabbles. French's tenure with the band was short-lived and consisted mainly of songwriting credits on their 1972 album '*Ot 'N' Sweaty*, before, depending on the version of the story, he was either shown the door due to yet another reconfiguration — in this case, the formation of Beck, Bogart & Appice — or left on his own accord.

Steve Bolton's post-Rooster career would last a bit longer. As part of the rock group Headstone, he contributed to two albums, *Bad Habits* and the self-titled *Headstone*, in the early seventies, as well as some live performances, before moving on to the next chapter of his career.

Chris Farlowe's time with Rooster was brief and, if discographies are accurate, it pretty much pushed him out of the spotlight, leaving him to pick up occasional solo or session gigs. Notably, he released the 1975 album *The Chris Farlowe Band Live* during this period.

Ric Parnell left Atomic Rooster and quickly found international success with the progressive rock Italian band Triton. When Triton's appeal waned, Parnell continued to develop his progressive chops with another European band, Ibis, and their album *Sun Supreme*. He eventually finished out his early seventies journey in a more commercial vein as part of the pop-rock group Stars.

With former band members venturing off in different directions and Crane seemingly in a state of mental hibernation, there appeared to be little left of the Atomic Rooster legacy to cling to. However, in 1975, a glimmer of recognition came with the release of the compilation album *Assortments*. Essentially a selection of tracks from Atomic Rooster's first three studio albums, it served as a solid reflection of what the band had been — and, under the right circumstances, what they still could be.

14
Vincent's Head Examined

On 8th May 1974, the mentally troubled organist Graham Bond was tragically run over by a train at Finsbury Park Station.

Bond, whose life had been marked by substance abuse and mental health struggles, had taken his own life. Various press reports also noted that in recent years, Bond had become increasingly obsessed with the occult.

In a grim twist of hindsight, it was observed that Bond and Crane shared many similarities.

At the time of Bond's death, Crane was desperately trying to keep some form of Atomic Rooster on the road. Financial pressures were likely a factor, but perhaps more tellingly, it seemed part of a manic effort to maintain his mental stability. Crane himself hinted at this in an interview, stating, "I don't think I could survive if I came off the road."

Crane's mental and emotional struggles were well known, even before his time with Atomic Rooster. In a tragic sense, they were a significant part of what drove him. It was often speculated that his bouts of dementia and depression were genetic, and that they were exacerbated by his time with The Crazy World of Arthur Brown and his LSD consumption. His wife, Pat, with her interest in the dark arts and spiritual bleakness, was also a major influence on Crane, guiding him down both creative and mental paths towards darker territories.

By the time Atomic Rooster found success, the pressures of being in the public eye only added to Crane's instability.

It became clear to everyone around him that Crane was struggling, with regular outbursts of anger and insecurity becoming part of the Atomic Rooster experience.

Poet and long-time friend of Crane, Paul Green, reflected on his attitude in *The Afterword*, saying, "The pressure of the music business often affected Vince in a worrying way. You could see it in his lyrics and his music. The concept of mortality was a constant companion that haunted him. Vincent read extensively in both Eastern and Western mysticism. Some of the pessimism in Atomic Rooster's lyrics may stem from the fact that some of the avenues he had hoped for in his perceived higher consciousness never materialised."

Peter French, who had always been diplomatic when discussing Crane's mental state, remained true to form and concise when asked to analyse it in *The Afterword*. "Vincent always had a mad act on stage, but offstage, his attitude didn't let much sunshine in."

Arthur Brown, who had known Crane for many years, also tried to be diplomatic when commenting on Crane's psyche in a conversation with *Hit Channel.com*. "Vincent was quite brilliant. Some people have that creative gift, and those people often have a different balance in their attitude. Vincent was what we now call bipolar. He could be really funny, telling jokes and making witty comments. But when he was on the manic side, he could be very difficult. He could occasionally be violent."

John Du Cann, in an excerpt from *Steve Hoffman's Music Forum.com*, got straight to the point in his assessment of Crane's ongoing mental state: "Vincent always had a bit of a mental problem. I remember him going into a mental hospital at least three times. It was the LSD that did it."

Barry Winton, a music journalist, avid record collector, and long-time friend of Crane's, witnessed his friend's mental unravelling in the seventies, as he explored the topic in *The Vinyl Hunter* documentary podcast on Atomic Rooster. "Vincent seemed to become increasingly closed off and paranoid. He was a genius, but as the saying goes, where there's genius, there is also madness. At times, he really couldn't help himself."

For those who knew him, the end of Atomic Rooster, coupled with the breakdown of his first marriage to Pat, marked the beginning of some dark days ahead.

Green, in *Steve Hoffman's Music Forum.com*, acknowledged that while Crane's erratic mental state was never in question, those who worked with him found ways to manage it. "In his more manic moments, Vincent had a great sense of humour. If you could connect with him on that level, you could get through to him. It was a bit like riding a very large motorcycle without brakes. But under the right conditions, it could be steered."

15
Wife Number Two

By the early 1970s, Crane's miserly attitude towards money was well known in both his personal and professional circles. It was assumed that even after disbanding Atomic Rooster, he was reasonably well off. However, that may not have been the case. Stories began to emerge suggesting that Crane was in significant debt and, in a manic state, had reportedly bricked up the front door of his residence in an attempt to prevent debt collectors from finding him.

Whether true or not, Crane's ongoing mental health struggles led to a rapid deterioration in his marriage to Pat. Little was known about their relationship, except for her interest in the occult, how it influenced Crane, and that she had received co-songwriting credit on four of the eight tracks of *In Hearing Of Atomic Rooster*. What is clear is that, off the road, Crane was not in an emotionally stable place, which undoubtedly affected their relationship.

It was during this period that Jean Lynam entered his life.

Starting at the age of sixteen, Lynam had worked her way up the London theatre scene, taking on roles as stage manager, sound engineer, and electrician on productions such as *The Killing Of Sister George, Jacques Brel Is Alive And Well And Living In Paris, Hair*, and *Cabaret*.

Lynam recalled in an interview in *Angel Fire.com* and *Lycos. com* how the two met, "When I first met Vincent, I was the sound engineer at The Roundhouse in London and Vincent had come on as musical director for The Red Buddha Theatre production of *Rain Dog*. When I first met Vincent, I had no idea who he was. I knew only that he was a very talented musician."

Working in close proximity on the production, it was inevitable that sparks would fly. They both had a mutual affection for the occult.

"I had been writing a lot of poetry and short stories and Vincent liked my work. Eventually we began writing together. I was a theatre person all my life and had no interest in rock and roll. But I knew that we were instantly attracted to each other."

The attraction quickly developed into a full-blown affair, creating some drama as Crane was still married. Eventually, Crane and Pat recognised the inevitable, and the couple divorced in 1976. Wasting little time in formalising their relationship, Crane and Lynam were married in 1977.

16
Not Missing In Action

For Crane, being without Atomic Rooster was an emotional rollercoaster.

He most likely missed the degree of notoriety and adulation that came with being in a popular band that always seemed on the verge of breaking through. If he was experiencing any self-pity or doubt, the now-idle musician kept it to himself.

However, likely with the encouragement and influence of his new wife Jean, Crane soon turned his attention to more diverse ventures to occupy his time. He composed the music for friend Paul Green's radio play *Ritual Of The Sifting Air*, which aired on Radio 2, and created the musical background for a production of *Dracula* at the Shaftesbury Theatre. He also found additional work scoring music for the plays *The Ghost Train*, *Old Country*, *Stevie* and *Rolls Hyphen Royce*.

Having something to challenge his creative talents gave Crane moments of accomplishment that helped soothe the absence of a regular gig fronting Atomic Rooster. Whenever he had even these relatively minor jobs, there was the occasional spark to be seen.

Perhaps his most meaningful creative stretch during this period came through a series of formal teaching roles. These included serving as musical advisor for the Royal Court Children's Theatre, vocal coach for the South London Children's Festival, and teaching recorder in a specialist class. Given Crane's eccentric personality, many who knew him expected something to go awry in his teaching work. But friend

Paul Green noted, "Vincent was quite proud of his teaching duties and was very professional, although he was not in the best mental health."

Crane also found time for more artistically fulfilling pursuits, continuing his role as musical director of the Red Buddha Theatre Company for *Rain Dog*, and participating in occasional jazz and poetry performances with Green.

During this period, Crane and Jean made what many considered a questionable decision: they took on a short lease for a group of dwellings that required refurbishment, with the risk of losing the lease if they failed. It was a tense time. As Paul Green explained, "It was a real crisis for Jean." In the end, however, Crane's patchwork of musical jobs pulled them through, and they became the proud owners of the property.

But the victory would prove short-lived, as Crane's increasingly frequent mental lapses continued to cast a shadow over their lives.

The musician's embrace of Irish politics, and in particular a local firefighters' strike, evolved into a one-man musical protest when—finances be damned — he pressed 5,000 copies of a political diatribe single titled 'Fire Fighter,' released under the nom de plume Green Goddess. Crane was convinced the record would single-handedly bring the firefighters' dispute to a screeching halt. However, 'Fire Fighter' failed to make much of an impact, with most of the copies ultimately given away in pubs. The disappointment plunged Crane into yet another deep depression, during which he became convinced that local politicians were conspiring against him.

But Crane was not to be denied in his rock and roll politicking. In another manic episode, he decided to form a band and tour Northern Ireland, aiming to bring what he saw as his revolutionary message to the fore. As recalled in a *CultureCourt.com* memoir narrated by Paul Green, Crane declared: "We've got to sort things out in Northern Ireland. I'm going to take a band over, set up a huge tour and entertain the armies, the troops, the whole fucking lot!"

Details of the tour are scarce, but what is known is that Crane returned from the experience in a remarkably good emotional state. This, in turn, led to an upturn in his musical fortunes in the mid-1970s, as he contributed some highly effective jazz, Latin, and funk stylings to Toni Verdi's solo album *Calypso*.

Heading into 1977, Vincent Crane appeared to be in a good place…

17
Among Other Things

...**S**o much so that he began reconnecting with past acquaintances — most notably, Arthur Brown. Whatever differences Crane and Brown may have had in the past were soon set aside, and the pair quickly turned their attention to the possibility of creating new music together. The result was an intriguing, though largely overlooked, project titled *Vincent Crane Featuring Arthur Brown: The Tarot Rota*.

The intent behind this seven-track album was never entirely clear. Was it a collaborative effort or essentially a Vincent Crane solo album? Further blurring the lines was the fact that Jeannie Crane received co-writing credits for several lyrics. The record included a surreal remake of Arthur Brown's 'Fire' and a re-imagined version of the Atomic Rooster track 'Black Snake,' both rendered in a bizarre mélange of musical and keyboard textures. While *The Tarot Rota* was never less than interesting, it was a wholly non-commercial release that failed to gain traction outside the most obscure corners of fandom.

What *The Tarot Rota* could have been was highlighted in an interview with Jeannie Crane on *AngelFire.com*:

"The piece we were working on in 1975 was a concept piece. *Tarot Rota* was based on the images of the Tarot cards. At the time, it was almost impossible to produce with piano and vocals. As it was conceived by Vincent, it ran for over twenty-two minutes and was fully orchestrated and arranged. It would have been too big for one side of a record. If only

Vincent had been able to complete this work the way we had first imagined it."

"I did an album with Arthur and we had a full orchestra and all sorts of things," Vincent recalled when talking to Paul Cole for the *Black Country Evening Mail* in 1980. "It sounded really good, but hasn't been released in England."

The creative chemistry between Crane and Brown would continue into 1977 with the release of *Chisholm In My Bosom*, arguably one of Brown's finest and most overlooked works. For Crane, *Chisholm* offered rich creative opportunity, allowing him to explore both sonic depth and subtlety. His contributions enhanced not only the more concise bursts of Brown's signature rock eccentricity but also the standout cover of 'I Put A Spell On You.'

However, lurking in the wider musical universe was a continued demand for anything bearing the name Atomic Rooster. This was demonstrated by the 1972 album *BBC Radio: Live In Concert*, which captured the band at its electrifying best. Another compilation, 1977's *Home To Roost*, served as a solid retrospective, compiling highlights from the band's first three albums.

Despite these reminders of past glories, Crane appeared determined to forge new musical paths. One such effort saw him and Arthur Brown contributing to Klaus Schulze's (the synthesiser virtuoso) entirely 'out there' fusion of electronic, space, and trance music on the album *Time Actor*, released under the pseudonym Richard Wahnfried on Schulze's Innovative Communications label in 1979. For Crane, the project was a boundless musical playground that enabled him to explore a variety of genres with complete creative freedom.

Impressed that Crane and Brown were, in his words, not "boring old farts," Schulze offered to release their next collaboration, *Faster Than The Speed Of Light*. The resulting album was a weighty and highly contemporary piece that explored themes of sanity and its loss. Brown provided the lyrics while Crane composed the music. The pairing — both artists known for delving into deep and often dark creative territory — produced a compelling and potent musical statement. Crane's sonically rich blend of prog rock and classical influences, in particular, received strong critical acclaim.

Faster Than The Speed Of Light saw a limited release in Germany and, unsurprisingly, sold only a small number of copies. However, it would go on to become a classic example of a critics' favourite, gradually building a cult reputation over the years.

Perhaps most importantly for Crane, the album and his previous late seventies side projects would both encourage and inspire him. Once again, he felt he was capable of great and mighty things. Once again, he was ready to give Atomic Rooster another go.

18
Did They Do It For The Money?

By the time 1980 rolled around, Crane had decided that the time was right to give Atomic Rooster another try. And to his way of thinking it made perfect sense. "I cut myself off from rock completely for three years. I'd been ten years on the road, and it was time for a rest," he told Paul Cole.

1980 marked a resurgence — a new wave, if you will — of hard rock and heavy metal, spearheaded by the likes of Iron Maiden, Judas Priest, and Def Leppard. These bands, to varying degrees, owed much to the musical foundations laid by Atomic Rooster.

There was also a more practical consideration: money. Even during times without new music or recording contracts, there remained a steady stream of live performance offers from clubs and festivals. Quite simply, regular gigs meant regular paycheques, and for Crane — who always seemed to be teetering on the edge of poverty — playing live was both a financial necessity and a psychological outlet.

Crane's initial plan was to reform Atomic Rooster with its most successful line-up: the classic power trio. Easier said than done, as this meant reconciling with guitarist John Du Cann, who, by that point, wasn't even on speaking terms with him. Nonetheless, Crane bit the bullet and phoned Du Cann with an offer to rejoin a revived Atomic Rooster.

Du Cann was interested, albeit cautious. He understood that while he and Crane could remain professional and possibly even cordial, they were unlikely to ever be close friends. Still, he agreed with the sentiment that Atomic Rooster had unfinished business. As he reflected in *Record Collector Magazine*, "There was unfinished business," he said. "The past is past. I just wanted to get out there and play the classics all over again."

To complete what was shaping up to be Atomic Rooster's most successful line-up, Crane attempted to bring back drummer Paul Hammond. Unfortunately, Hammond was by then deep in the grip of full-blown alcoholism and unfit for the demands of recording and touring. Crane instead turned to session drummer Preston Heyman.

Adding to the momentum was renewed label interest — EMI stepped in with a $30,000 offer to sign the band and record a brand-new album. The resulting self-titled release, *Atomic Rooster*, was recorded in mid-1980.

Following a five-year hiatus — and the lingering disappointment of *Made In England* — Atomic Rooster re-emerged with a rough and ready hard rock sound, blending classic elements of the band's earlier style with a well-judged nod to the prevailing hard rock and heavy metal scene.

Co-produced by Crane and Du Cann, the album featured two reworked tracks from Du Cann's 1977 solo effort *The World Is Not Big Enough* — 'She's My Woman' and 'Where's the Show?' — and was powered by the vintage-sounding single 'Do You Know Who's Looking For You?' Atomic Rooster was back, and in solid, hard-rocking form.

Writing for the *Manchester Evening News*, Ray King said of the album, "The name may be out of the past but there's no cobwebs on Atomic Rooster '80. Frantic hard rock with searing guitars and keyboards blow the dust away."

Things were looking good. A series of warm-up gigs with the new/old line-up were met with much excitement and a full-blown tour was quickly put together.

"We've played some quiet gigs to make sure it works," said Crane. "We played our first big gig at the Music Machine in London. It seemed as if we'd got our old audience back again, but there were still lots of youngsters asking for songs that were probably written before they'd ever heard a live rock band."

It appeared that the return of Atomic Rooster was poised for success.

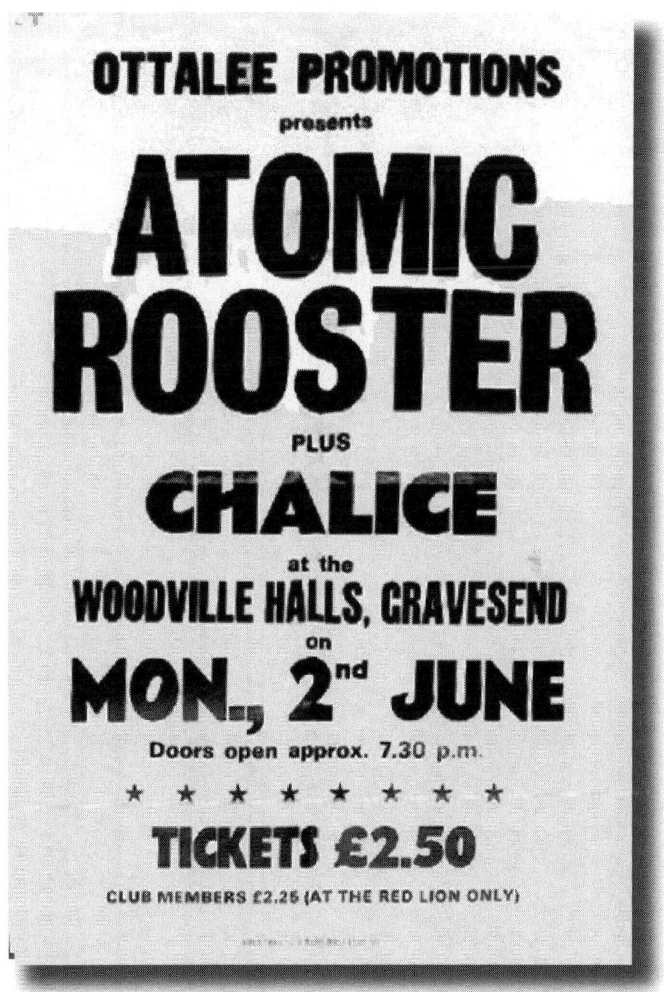

19
Rooster Is Snake-Bit

Preston Heyman was constantly in demand and had already committed to a string of gigs well into the future — even as he was agreeing to join Atomic Rooster. This, unsurprisingly, did not bode well for the band's plans.

As a result, legendary Cream drummer Ginger Baker entered the fold. The chronology of Baker's involvement is somewhat murky. EMI Records claimed that he was already confirmed to replace Heyman before the 1980 tour began. In addition to previously reported comments from his daughter Nettie — who noted that he was both financially strapped and struggling with drug addiction — Baker had recently disbanded his latest group, Energy, and was in urgent need of a paying gig. To him, joining Rooster appeared to be a mercenary move to secure some quick income.

What is known for certain is that Baker's time with Atomic Rooster was brief — lasting only a couple of weeks and a handful of gigs — before, depending on varying accounts, he was either dismissed by Crane or chose to leave of his own accord.

Whilst Baker was still on board, James Belsey reported in the *Bristol Evening Post* in August of a "little-publicised" warm-up gig near Glastonbury that apparently drew a crowd of more than a thousand.

With a lucrative European tour scheduled well into 1981, one of Preston Heyman's prior commitments resurfaced in the form of a Kate Bush recording session — an opportunity he simply couldn't refuse. Heyman jumped ship, leaving Atomic Rooster high and dry.

Once again in urgent need of a drummer, Crane turned to Paul Hammond. Although Hammond's alcoholism remained a significant concern, a quick rehearsal-cum-audition suggested he was in sufficient shape to handle the demands of touring, and he was reinstated in the band.

Reports from the early dates of the tour were mixed. The prospect of Atomic Rooster's classic line-up reuniting and performing live sparked considerable curiosity and resulted in well-attended shows. However, early reviews suggested that the band may have returned to the stage prematurely. Performances were frequently marred by technical issues and Hammond's struggles in a live setting, widely attributed to insufficient rehearsal time.

David Blows, for the *Hull Daily Mail* on 29th September, wrote about a gig at Scarborough Penthouse, reporting: "Former Cream drummer Ginger Baker was expected to join the band but was sacked because 'he couldn't keep up,' and album drummer Preston Heyman was brought in. But after a handful of concerts he left, and Hammond unexpectedly returned."

Commenting on the gig itself, Blows observed: "With the original Rooster crowing again, the midnight soiree, with about 500 fans, should have exploded in nostalgia and anticipation. But the band were plagued with sound problems, the virtually unrehearsed Hammond, and new material which doesn't have the raw power of the old Atomic Rooster. It had the nuclear energy but not the spark to ignite it."

"It was an uphill struggle, even during the classic 'Tomorrow's Night,' so the concert was patchy and largely disappointing. The band still erupt in that singularly original style of heavy rock that set Atomic Rooster apart from other bands — it just needs tightening up."

By early October 1980, following gigs at the Tameside Theatre, The Marquee and Maximillians, the band continued to perform in a workmanlike fashion — at times offering glimpses of the Atomic Rooster that had made their mark across three albums. Unfortunately, while the new album was solid enough, it failed to show the commercial potential EMI had been hoping for. The label quickly grew frustrated with the band's lack of commercial success and, by 1981 — midway through the tour — dropped Atomic Rooster from its roster.

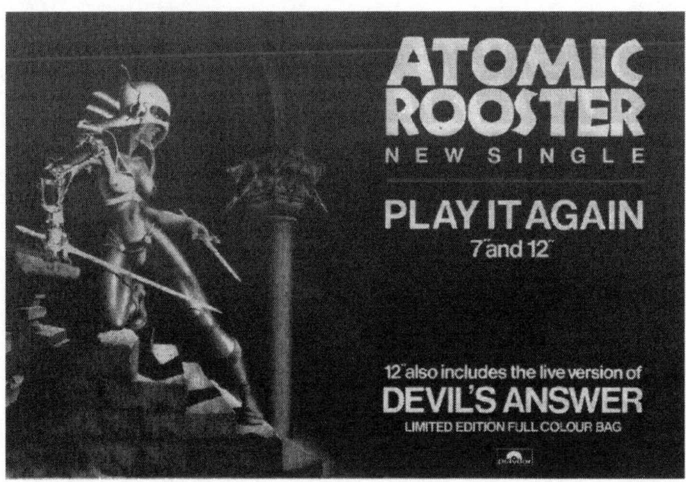

20
Crane Sings While Rooster Burns

Not long after being dropped by EMI, long-time friend Paul Green and his partner had the opportunity to move into a multi-unit building owned by Crane and Jeannie, where they were living at the time. Despite expectations that Crane might fall into another prolonged mental slump, Green recalled in *Culture Court.com* that, at least on the surface, Crane appeared to be in good spirits.

"In the evenings, there was often lavish hospitality in Vince and Jean's apartment, with impromptu jams, readings, parties, and performances."

During his stay at the Crane residence, Green would often wake up in the middle of the night to the loud strains of classical music and show tunes, accompanied by Crane singing along passionately. "Every morning for weeks, we've heard Vincent working out on selections of Gilbert & Sullivan. He insisted it was excellent for improving vocal control and diction."

The more likely explanation was that the spontaneous and wide-ranging thinker was testing whether he was up to taking on vocal duties within the band if needed.

This period of relative peace at home coincided with the usual chaos surrounding Atomic Rooster.

In 1981, the band signed a straightforward deal with Polydor Records for the release of two exploratory singles and, ideally, a follow-up album. The singles, 'Play It Again' and 'End Of Day,' were solid examples of prog rock that proved popular in a live setting but ultimately failed to chart.

The fate of the song 'Play It Again' was particularly frustrating, reflecting the bad karma that seemed to follow the group. As Du Cann recalled in *Steve Hoffman's Music Forums*: "The single 'Play It Again' had enough pre-orders to chart at No. 16 in the UK. But the record pressing plant decided to go on strike at that point and couldn't produce enough copies to meet the pre-orders. At that stage, Polydor gave priority to Siouxsie And The Banshees. So, our song didn't get pressed in enough quantity to fulfil the pre-order quota."

Despite these commercial setbacks, the band continued to be a popular live act, playing clubs and occasional festivals. While still struggling to secure paying gigs, a core group of Rooster fans ensured the band remained somewhat visible in the public eye.

The internal chemistry of the band, particularly between Crane and Du Cann, was fragile at best.

Du Cann, ever candid, acknowledged the growing tension in an interview with *Record Collector Magazine*, revealing that the rivalry and bickering had reached breaking point. "I really had just about enough and wanted out. Simple as that."

For a time, Du Cann managed to set aside his differences with Crane and continued to play with Atomic Rooster. The reality was, as emotionally draining as dealing with Crane had become, it was still a gig that paid the bills, and at that point, Du Cann didn't have a better offer.

However, everything changed in 1982 when Atomic Rooster was scheduled to perform at the prestigious three-day Reading Festival. The event, featuring acts like Billy Squier, The Kinks, Wishbone Ash, Girlschool, and Budgie, was a major opportunity. Atomic Rooster was booked for an early afternoon set. That was when Du Cann failed to show up. The reasons behind his absence remain unclear to this day, but what was certain was that Crane wasn't about to cancel an important gig. Within a day, Mick Hawksworth (Andromeda) was brought in as a replacement guitarist.

Atomic Rooster managed to salvage the Reading appearance, but it was the last straw for Du Cann, who was immediately fired. Adding insult to injury, Polydor, impatient with the lack of commercial success and the ongoing drama within the band, dropped Atomic Rooster from the label.

21
A Curious Side Project

If you blinked, you might have missed this obscure Vincent Crane side project called *A Case For The Blues*, recorded by a group named Katmandu. Here's how it unfolded:

In 1983, Peter Green, formerly of Fleetwood Mac, was looking to try something a little different — and, hopefully, lucrative. He met Ray Dorset, the former frontman of Mungo Jerry, and the two hit it off. Informal meetings and conversations soon turned into something more concrete when a company with financial backing offered $120,000 to fund rehearsals and the recording of an album.

Both Green and Dorset had heard of Vincent Crane and his reputation as a talented lyricist and musical arranger. With Atomic Rooster languishing after its dismissal by Polydor, Crane was eager to find a new challenge that could bring in some income. They enlisted musician Jeff Whitaker, and Katmandu was born.

The band set about recording *A Case For The Blues*, a vibrant mix of rhythm & blues, soul, and Afro-Cuban music. The sessions were laid-back and easygoing, with everyone getting along well. Even the notoriously difficult Crane was more cooperative than usual. For the record, Crane received writing credits for 'Crane's Train Boogie' and 'Sweet Sixteen,' and a co-writing credit for 'Who's That Knocking.'

Dorset, always seemingly up for a party-like atmosphere, found the ideal compatriot in Crane, as he observed in an extract from *The Afterword*. "Vincent and me, we got on like a house on fire. We shared the same sense of humour and had such a great laugh together. He smoked a lot of grass but he was very speedy. I guess the grass slowed down the manic side of him. But then it probably added to his paranoia."

Dorset recalled, "I had met Peter once before in 1970 on a visit to a music store in New York when we'd had a nice chat but within a few years he had become a recluse after going through some of the worst traumas you could imagine. People reckoned that his brain had gone as the result of some heavy substance abuse which was not helped when his drink was spiked with LSD during a tour of America."

Dorset described Green as "a very sensitive person who had been diagnosed with schizophrenia and what happened with the LSD affected him so much he was institutionalised for a time. He tried to give all his money away and took jobs as a gravedigger and a hospital porter. He also let his fingernails grow so long that he could no longer play his guitar."

Dorset continued, "However, by the late 1970s he had begun recording solo albums again. I met Chris Holland (Green's then tour manager), who said to me: 'How would you like to have a jam with Peter?' which I thought would be great! Chris told me that percussionist Jeff Whittaker, who was working with Green and who had previously worked with Pink Floyd's Dave Gilmour, would probably be interested in joining us and that he'd call me to set it up. Chris called a few days later to say that he had been on Richard Branson's boat and had met Vincent Crane who was also interested in joining the session."

Unfortunately, what had the potential to be an exciting musical venture for all involved fell apart shortly after the completion of the album, reportedly due to disagreements over finances. As a result, Katmandu disbanded before it truly had a chance to begin. After some time, *A Case For The Blues* — the first of several releases of the album over the years — was eventually released in 1985.

22
A Recipe For Success?

Crane's mind was always brimming with ideas, and he was never one to keep them to himself. Such was the case in 1982 when he and his good friend, Cream songwriter Pete Brown, got together. Brown recalled the conversation: "Vincent said, 'I've got this great setup, man,' and I asked, 'What is it?' He replied, 'Well, I've got this house, and downstairs from my flat there's this great rehearsal room, and upstairs my dealer lives.' I thought, 'Yeah, that's really great, Vincent. A recipe for success.'"

At this point in his life, Crane's ideas came at a rather precarious time. He was without a label deal, had no band to speak of, and it seemed as though Atomic Rooster was once again headed for extinction. However, as Jeannie Crane recalled in an interview for her homepage, the mantra "never say never" was always in play.

"Tom Newman lived up the road from us. We didn't know him before, but we always joked as we walked past his house that it would be wonderful if the mobile studio parked outside could be brought down the road for us to record an album at our home. That's when Vincent managed to land a record deal with a small label called Towerbell Records to make an album. Then, surprise, surprise, that's exactly what happened."

The result was the album *Headline News*. Depending on your perspective, *Headline News* could be considered either an Atomic Rooster album or a Vincent Crane solo album. Paul Green, a close friend of Crane's who at the time was living in an upper floor of the Crane household, had a front-row seat to the creation of *Headline News*. He recalled that Crane described the new album as being different from his earlier works, mentioning more subtle and unexpected moods and textures. In essence, it was to be a departure from anything he had done before.

To begin with, the only person other than Vincent Crane who had any connection to an Atomic Rooster album was drummer Paul Hammond. The rest of the musicians were, for the most part, local — either from down the street or, figuratively, around the block. The list of musicians and singers who came in and out of the *Headline News* sessions included John Mizarolli, former Gillan guitarist Bernie Tormé, Tareena Craze (a member of the choir on one track), John Field, Jean Crane (who not only wrote the lyrics for three songs but also sang in the choir on one track), and, most significantly, David Gilmour.

Jean Crane reflected on the ad-hoc nature of the recording process on her website: "It was released as an Atomic Rooster album, but it was very much a solo album for Vincent. He laid down all the basic tracks himself on his piano with a drum machine. We then took the tracks to Paul Hammond to record the drums and percussion, and to David Gilmour's studio for the guitar parts. Tom [Newman] knew Dave very well and had introduced us to him. We were delighted when he agreed to play on some of the tracks himself."

The informal and freewheeling nature of the recording process also extended to the musicians involved, particularly Bernie Tormé, who described it as a great experience in an interview with *DMME.net*. "It was great fun. Musically, it was always very challenging. Vincent Crane was a great musician to work with. I didn't meet David Gilmour at the time — he'd recorded his parts before me. As it turned out, one of my solos was used in place of one of his. Tom Newman preferred it, which turned out to be a real feather in my cap."

Despite its seemingly low-key production, *Headline News* would prove, in hindsight, to be a positive experience. Jean Crane was quick to emphasise the psychological and emotional benefits of the time spent making the album on her homepage: "It became one of the most enjoyable times ever. We were all over the place with the mobile studio making the album, and on days off, they'd play impromptu blues gigs at our local pub. Anybody and everybody would drop in, and a wonderful time was had by all."

126

23
If It Wasn't For Bad Luck

1st February 1983. The dark confines of the Zeche Club in Bochum, Germany. The latest incarnation of Atomic Rooster — Vincent Crane, Bernie Tormé, and Paul Hammond — take the stage. The band was on fire that night, blending classic tracks with newer material, just as they always had. This particular gig was notable for a poorly recorded, single-microphone recording of the set, which, years later, would resurface on Tormé's own label, RetroWrek, as the live album *Live In Germany 1983*. However, on the night of the gig, there was more happening than just another Atomic Rooster show.

The band had been touring fairly steadily since completing *Headline News*, primarily in Germany, Italy, and the UK, building momentum ahead of the album's release in June 1983. In May 1983, a month before the album hit the shelves, the band released their first single in years, 'Land Of Freedom.' The track was a crunchy blend of prog-pop with a commercial, rocking instrumental edge. Unfortunately, the single failed to chart, which was disappointing. However, Crane and the band still held out hope that better days would come with the album's release.

Sadly, *Headline News* was essentially dead on arrival. Reviews were mixed, ranging from outright dismissive to intriguingly different in a way that didn't align with Atomic Rooster's established sound. The fact that the album sold almost nothing was only part of the bad luck that plagued Crane and the band. *Music Week* and other rock publications reported that, almost simultaneously with the album's release, Towerbell Records declared bankruptcy, citing "cash flow problems" and "meetings with creditors." As Jean Crane recalled in an interview on her homepage, the label's collapse was deeply personal for the band.

"Unfortunately, just after the album was released, our record label, Towerbell, went bankrupt. All the money disappeared to South America along with a certain gentleman and his secretary. Having never seen any statements or received any money from the original release, I had no idea how many albums were sold and where."

Not surprisingly, Crane was unhappy, and in the following months, he slipped back into bouts of manic depression. For a time, he soldiered on with Atomic Rooster, playing enough live gigs in the strongholds of Germany and Italy. However, as the shows continued, Crane increasingly complained that the quality of musicianship within the band had plummeted. Eventually, he reached his breaking point.

By the end of 1983, Crane announced that he was disbanding Atomic Rooster once again.

24
Just About Midnight

During their time together, Jeannie had seen Vincent at his worst and had learned that the best way to care for her husband was to be supportive and encouraging. However, she wasn't prepared for the deep gloom that settled in after the latest break-up of Atomic Rooster.

Day after day, month after month, Crane would sit for hours at his piano, practising and mentally berating himself for not being a better musician. For Jean, it was a difficult sight. Late in 1983, she came across an ad in *Melody Maker*. A 'name band' was looking for musicians with soul. It didn't take long for her to deduce that the 'name band' was Dexys Midnight Runners, a soul/pop group that had enjoyed significant commercial success throughout the early-to-mid-eighties. However, creative differences and personnel changes had left band leader Kevin Rowland searching for a new direction and new members.

Jean approached her husband with the ad, suggesting it might be worth exploring. Crane readily agreed, seeing the opportunity to simply be a member of the band rather than deal with the stress of hiring, firing, and decision-making that had weighed on him as the head of Atomic Rooster.

For Rowland, the equation was simple: he needed great players to make a great album. But it wasn't as easy as it sounded. There were several near-misses during the recruiting process — musicians with the right amount of soul, but who couldn't quite take Rowland's vision to the next level. That was until, as Rowland recalled in *The Afterword*, "Helen, the person handling the early auditions, called and said, 'I think you should see this guy.'"

This guy was Vincent Crane.

Rowland and Crane quickly hit it off. Crane was hired and immediately immersed in Rowland's vision. On the surface, the album that would become *Don't Stand Me Down* seemed commercially impossible. It was to be a group effort, recorded live, with no clear hint of a potential hit single. Rowland soon realised that Crane was the perfect fit for the project. "The day we started recording, Vince said, 'This has to be right. This could be another *Dark Side Of The Moon*.' He really understood it. He just got it. You didn't have to tell him what to play. He heard the song and just got inside it."

Don't Stand Me Down was released on 13th September 1985. Critically and commercially, the album was doomed to fail on several fronts. Crane's involvement with the band continued post-*Don't Stand Me Down*, as he remained part of Dexys Midnight Runners' touring line-up from 1985 to 1987. One thing was certain: when Crane was in his element, whether recording or touring, there was no doubt about his professionalism.

Yet, the dark days would continue to haunt him.

25
It's Great Being Mad

Chris Farlowe has never been one to mince his words. He was particularly succinct in his assessment of Vincent Crane's mental state when speaking with *Music2Stay.de*: "Vincent Crane was a lovely man, but he was very screwed up."

With little to distract him musically in the mid-eighties, his manic depression began to escalate. There were early signs of Crane's decline during the making of *Don't Stand Me Down*, when Dexys leader Kevin Rowland noted that Crane would occasionally get into seemingly unreasonable arguments over minor disagreements.

During this period, Crane's mental disarray led to an affair with a Swiss stripper named Katisha. Far from keeping it private, Crane had no qualms about going public, even introducing Katisha to his parents on one occasion.

Paul Green witnessed this very public affair and sympathised with Katisha, who found herself caught in the middle of Crane's madness. "She had gone along with Vincent's manic euphoria, believing she had met a man who had been in a number one band. But along the way, she discovered that he had a wife."

Crane's deteriorating mental state led to multiple stays in mental hospitals over the next couple of years. Green was present during some of these episodes, when Crane, in his most manic moments, would extol the virtues of being unhinged. "Vincent would say, 'You know, it's great being mad. You really ought to try it. You walk into restaurants and don't pay for meals, and you wake up in bed with strange women.'"

Given Crane's deepening mental deterioration and his infidelity, it was no surprise that his marriage to Jean was on the rocks. Though they tried to keep their relationship intact, it always seemed on the verge of collapse.

Between 1985 and 1987, Crane's life fluctuated between spontaneous, maddening episodes. At one point, he could be found busking on the city streets as a juggler. Through this, he began spending more and more time with street people, junkies, and winos.

At his most delusional, Crane would often wildly speculate about yet another incarnation of Atomic Rooster. Sadly, those who heard his grand plans took them as flights of mad fancy, not to be taken seriously.

Chris Farlowe had not seen Crane for some time, but when they unexpectedly crossed paths in early 1988, it was a painful revelation. Farlowe recalled the encounter: "I hadn't seen him in years. I was walking through a flea market when I saw him, standing there with all his clothes spread out on the pavement. I asked, 'What are you doing here?' He said, 'I'm selling my clothes.' I asked why, and he replied, 'I'm broke. I have nothing. My wife has left me.'"

For Farlowe, the scene was heartbreaking. "I felt so fucking bad about it."

26
The Last Gigs Of Crane On Earth

By 1987, people would have been justified in asking, "Atomic Rooster who?" "Vincent Crane who?"

Crane's ongoing mental decline had increasingly isolated him, and there was a noticeable absence of even a greatest hits or compilation album to spark any memories. However, even at his lowest points, there were brief flashes of activity from Crane. He had managed to maintain a cordial relationship with guitarist John Mizarolli following the *Headline News* sessions.

In a 1987 interview with *Guitarist Magazine*, Mizarolli alluded to this. "I played for a while with Atomic Rooster, laying down tracks on three *Headline News* songs, and at the moment, I'm working with Vincent on recording some demos — most notably Crane's keyboard runs on the song 'Tibet' — to get record companies interested in releasing a new solo album of mine, *Gigging With The Angels*."

During this period, there were reports that Crane had been writing songs for pop rocker Kim Wilde. However, if anything came of that collaboration, it was never fully confirmed, and no songs credited to Crane appeared on Wilde's subsequent albums.

There were also reports that, in his more lucid moments, Crane would occasionally visit a local pub for some informal jamming. Into 1988, his recurring thoughts of getting Atomic

Rooster back together suddenly seemed plausible. Crane had reconnected with John Du Cann and, in principle, agreed to reunite the band for another attempt. A tour was quickly organised, according to *Artists Camp.com*, which would see Atomic Rooster touring Germany with The Edgar Broughton Band.

At this point, however, Crane succumbed to yet another depressive setback, pushing him so far from reality that the tour was ultimately cancelled.

27
A Lovely Warm Damaged Man

Veteran music journalist Mark Paytress effectively conducted the final interview with Vincent Crane. In an excerpt that appeared in *Record Collector Magazine*, he painted a portrait of Crane as a tragic figure, one whose story went far beyond the typical rock and roll narrative of excess and ego.

At one point, Paytress described the musician as "a lovely, warm, damaged man." As 1989 approached, this description seemed all too fitting. Crane was enduring a particularly difficult period, repeatedly telling anyone who would listen that he had let everyone in his life down, both personally and professionally, and that he saw no hope for his future. The small, dwindling group of people left in his life feared the worst.

Barry Winton, a long-time friend of Crane, recounted in *The Vinyl Hunters* documentary on Crane and Atomic Rooster how he went to Crane's house on 14th February to check on him. "I spoke to him briefly. He seemed a bit distracted, so I didn't stay long. A bit later, I called him, but got no answer."

What Winton didn't know was that Crane had been stockpiling boxes of the painkiller Anadin — reportedly more than 400 pills — and had taken them all. Winton later recalled the moment he discovered Crane's body and learned of his successful suicide. "It must have been a horrible way to die," he said.

The cold hard facts: Vincent Crane died from a deliberate overdose at the age of forty-five.

His death rocked the music world, though in some ways, it didn't come as a complete shock. There were the usual sympathy notices, remembrances, and, even in death, the word 'underrated' was frequently used to describe him. Vincent Crane never truly received the respect he deserved.

28
The Rooster At Rest

The suicide of Vincent Crane officially brought the saga of Atomic Rooster to an end. Or did it?

Long-time fans of the band — through memories and reflections posted across countless web pages — kept the history and legend of Atomic Rooster alive. Inevitably, there were calls for any unreleased material: rarities, outtakes and demos that surely had to be lying untouched in basements or vaults. Jeannie Crane, now the de facto custodian of Atomic Rooster's legacy, heard those calls and was quick to offer a reality check. "Vincent only ever worked up his songs when he had an album to make. All I have of any new material is on cassette, and it is unfinished."

Unsurprisingly, the end of Atomic Rooster — particularly in light of Crane's death — would live on through a flood of compilations, live recordings, and box sets of varying scope and quality released between 1992 and 2011.

What proved most illuminating amid this resurgence was the renewed focus on the band's origins and their first three albums — widely regarded as the high-water mark of Atomic Rooster's popularity and critical standing, when they were viewed as a rising live force with genuine superstar potential.

From *Made In England* onward, however, critical response became increasingly dismissive. These later releases were often seen as afterthoughts, with occasional discs drawing attention only to what many perceived as half-hearted efforts. The prevailing view suggested that Atomic Rooster had either coasted on early glories or, worse, slipped into a steady decline.

There remained, however, a deep sense of nostalgia and longing — for what Atomic Rooster once was and what it might have become. This feeling was particularly poignant during the band's extended absence, marked by the death of drummer Paul Hammond in 1992 and, perhaps more significantly, the passing of John Du Cann in 2011, whom many regarded as the true driving force behind the band's success.

For many, Atomic Rooster was now truly at rest — survived only by the memories.

29
They've Come For The Rooster

The idea of bringing back Atomic Rooster in some form had been a persistent topic of conversation among fans for years.

No one could deny that, at their peak, the band was more than worth the price of admission. They were consistently excellent in a live setting and, despite some questionable decisions, their albums generally stood as strong examples of what good progressive rock should sound like.

From a business perspective, the name Atomic Rooster still carried some financial clout. And among the many musicians who had passed through the band's various incarnations, few had anything negative to say about the quality of the music the group had produced. The musicians, too, had heard the call to revive the Rooster.

In particular, Steve Bolton remembered the moment clearly, as he recalled in conversation with the author:

"Reforming Atomic Rooster is something that had been knocking on my door for a while. At some point, I called Pete French and talked to him. We agreed that getting Atomic Rooster back together was a good idea."

French, speaking to *Classic Rock*, dispelled the often-repeated claim that it was he — rather than Bolton — who initiated the band's revival. "It all happened in a bizarre way.

Steve Bolton heard a rumour that somebody was planning a new Atomic Rooster line-up, and he came to me and suggested that we do it ourselves."

It was an idea that required taking the proposal to Crane's widow, Jean, who — following Vincent's death — had become the gatekeeper of anything related to Atomic Rooster. In short order, Jean granted permission for a new incarnation of the band to move forward. Bolton acknowledged that this was not a decision taken lightly.

"We decided to play a couple of test gigs to see how it would go and to test the waters."

French explained that caution was integral to their aim of making this new version of Atomic Rooster feel legitimate.

"I love that the goal was to bring new life to songs that, otherwise, might not be heard. I can feel the presence of Vincent and John in the back of my mind. It's like they were giving us the seal of approval. But I'd like to think that what we were going to do on stage was our own thing."

With French and Bolton leading the reunion, the new Atomic Rooster line-up was rounded out with the addition of Christian Madden (keyboards), Shug Millidge (bass), and Bo Walsh (drums).

Walsh, in an email exchange with the author, revealed that he was invited to join Atomic Rooster through his friendship with Madden. The invitation brought back vivid memories.

"I always remembered the artwork of Atomic Rooster albums from when I was a kid, seeing the album sleeves in my dad's record shop. I would look at those covers and think this stuff was weird as fuck."

Walsh's appreciation for the band's legacy deepened during his audition. "Listening to the albums and learning the parts, I found the music just as strange and yet musically enticing enough to want to get involved. The music was fun to play and I think it really suited my style of drumming. I couldn't help but feel at the time that I had actually joined Spinal Tap."

The reformed Atomic Rooster made their official return on 14th July 2016 with a warm-up gig in Clitheroe, Lancashire. Their setlist would become a reliable staple, blending generous selections from the band's first three albums, the occasional track from the *Made In England* period, and a showstopper in homage to Vincent Crane's days with The Crazy World of Arthur Brown — 'Fire.'

As it turned out, this incarnation of Atomic Rooster proved to be the right band at the right time. Over the next three years, they played to enthusiastic crowds at venues such as the 100 Club, the Eel Pie Club, and Under The Bridge, while also securing prime spots on festival stages, including HRH Prog V in Pwllheli and Weyfest in Farnham.

Within this context, drummer Bo Walsh had a front-row seat to the band's internal chemistry, echoing that of earlier eras.

"Steve Bolton and Pete French were both touching seventy at that time, yet still emphasised that iconic rock and roll flair. Both could still play and sing like fuck. At times they came across as very different characters and often rubbed each other the wrong way, much to the amusement of the rest of the band. But they always remained consummate professionals."

Walsh also recalled the unpredictable, fly-by-the-seat-of-their-pants energy that sometimes defined this version of the band — such as a mad dash from Munich to Kraków, Poland, to make a festival appearance.

"I arrived at the festival literally as Rooster was about to go onstage. I stepped out of the cab and someone stuck a pair of drumsticks in my hand and, with no rehearsal time, onstage I went."

Despite consistent praise for their live performances, old inconsistencies once again began to surface. Less than a year into the revival, Christian Madden was let go and replaced by Adrian Gautrey — a true triple threat on keyboards and guitar, and a decent vocalist to boot. By 2019, Pete French's well-known tendency to resist any musical direction that wasn't his own re-emerged, and an announcement was made that he was leaving Atomic Rooster. That announcement, however, proved premature, and a follow-up confirmed that French was back in the fold.

Walsh, meanwhile, remained with the band until 2020,

when he departed for greener pastures. He was succeeded by Paul Everette.

By that point, the band had become rock solid, made up of musicians genuinely committed to the long haul. Atomic Rooster was officially back in the game — and as Walsh summed it up, his time with the group was "a whole lot of fun."

30
Into The Future

Between 2020 and 2024, Atomic Rooster continued to defy the odds and the expectations often levelled at a band long past its prime and seemingly clinging on by the proverbial thread.

Touring fairly regularly — particularly capitalising on the enduring support of their fan bases in the UK, Italy, and Germany — the band, now regarded by critics as a journeyman, second-tier act, had become a legitimate top-notch live attraction.

Their setlist, now a familiar blend of long-lost greatest hits and powerful album favourites, provided the band not only with the opportunity to revisit past creative glories but also to inject new energy and perspective into their performance.

Remarkably, they were hitting a peak without having released a new album — or any new music at all — in over two decades. There was nothing fresh to boost their commercial appeal or, crucially, improve the ever-important bottom line.

All of that changed in 2024. During an interview with the author, Steve Bolton casually dropped a bombshell: Atomic Rooster had recently been in the studio. Would the author be interested in hearing some of the demos from those sessions?

Needless to say, the response was an emphatic yes. Shortly afterwards, Bolton sent over files containing half a dozen new Atomic Rooster songs.

Based on these demos — and imagining an alternative

timeline in which Crane had stayed on the creative trajectory that led up to and included *In Hearing Of Atomic Rooster*, perhaps even begrudgingly following John Du Cann's lead — what unfolds here has the makings of a logical and, in many ways, smarter and more calculated fourth album. Everything that defines the expectations of progressive rock, and the essential touchstones of what Atomic Rooster once stood for before their critical decline, is here in abundance.

The rich, flowing keyboard textures, interwoven with raw, tasteful guitar passages, move effortlessly through the expected melancholy and introspective lyrics. This incarnation of Atomic Rooster has clearly learned well from its past. These songs serve as a textbook example of building on what came before and pushing it forward. All things considered; the demos are a strong indication that anything new to emerge from the current line-up is full of promise.

For now, however, it remains a matter of speculation.

As of early 2025, according to a follow-up email from Bolton, the band still had no label deal in place. However, that changed quickly. As reported by outlets such as *Progressive Rock Journal*, Atomic Rooster not only confirmed the first in a series of 2025 live appearances but also revealed that they had been in the recording studio — and that the result, the first album of original Atomic Rooster material since *Headline News*, was now firmly on the horizon.

31
All Hail
The Imperfect Beast

When Vincent Crane was interviewed by the BBC around the time of the release of the very first Atomic Rooster album, he hesitated when asked: "What exactly is Atomic Rooster?" You could almost see him mentally stuttering and searching for an answer. Eventually, he ventured, "I guess what you could call what we do prog rock."

While the music has always been the driving force — keeping fans engaged through a story that at times reads like a progressive Greek tragedy — Atomic Rooster is a band that has weathered turmoil, tragedy, ego and madness in staggering proportions. And yet, it has come through it all: battle-scarred and bloodied, but unbowed. This endurance is thanks, in no small part, to the calibre of musicians who have passed through the band's revolving doors over the years — through albums and tours alike — always a consistently professional and dedicated group.

You've now seen the ups, downs, and all-arounds of a band that might have achieved global recognition, had the fates and the gods of popular music been kinder. Yet, as we enter 2025, Atomic Rooster — still the imperfect beast — remains very much alive and kicking. If you find yourself watching them perform in a small, darkened room or on a festival stage before thousands, count yourself lucky.

Because good music is timeless.

And the next chapter of Atomic Rooster is just around the corner.

Epilogue
Here Comes The Sun

In early March 2025, just as the author was rounding the clubhouse turn on *Atomic Rooster*, it was announced that the first album of new material since *Headline News* would be released in the summer.

For the sake of timeliness, I tracked down Steve Bolton for an update. As of this moment, the album is entitled *Circle The Sun*. In an email exchange — sent from, where else, somewhere on the road — Bolton confirmed that *Circle The Sun* had been recorded live, with only the bare minimum of overdubs.

"What can I say?" enthused Bolton. "We are very pleased with the album. It is a true Atomic Rooster album. Folks that have heard tracks are astounded. This album sounds like classic Atomic Rooster — plus so much more."

To prove his point, Bolton sent over files containing two tracks from *Circle The Sun*. It was early morning, and the first cup of coffee had barely kicked in — but the author couldn't help himself. He slipped on the headphones. No brag. No hype. Just fact.

You've got to love a happy ending.

Appendices
Discography

One would have to look far back to find a band with a history as chequered as Atomic Rooster's — and even then, few can boast more vinyl releases to their name than the average person has fingers and toes. But where there are devoted fans, there is always a market, and Atomic Rooster has been no exception. For diehard followers, many of these titles will be familiar. Yet, lurking in the vinyl undergrowth, there may well be one or two obscurities guaranteed to drive completists to distraction.

Singles

Friday The 13th / Banstead (1970)
Tomorrow Night / Play The Game (1970)
Devil's Answer / The Rock (1971)
Save Me / Close Your Eyes (1972)
Stand By Me / Never To Lose (1972)
Tell Your Story (Sing Your Song) / O. D. (1974)
Do You Know Who's Looking For You? / Throw Your Life Away (1980)
Devil's Answer / Tomorrow Night / Can't Take No More (1980)
Play It Again / Start To Live (1981)
End Of The Day / Living Underground (1982)
Land Of Freedom / Carnival (1983)
Devil's Answer / Tomorrow Night (1984)
No More / Rebel Devil (2024)
(The first new tracks since 1983, both from the forthcoming album. Also Includes live tracks from 2023: 'VUG,' 'Blacksnake,' 'A Spoonful Of Bromide,' 'Decision / Indecision.')

Studio Albums

Atomic Roooster (1970)
Death Walks Behind You (1970)
In Hearing Of Atomic Rooster (1971)
Made In England (1972)
Nice 'n' Greasy (1973)
Atomic Rooster (1980)
Headline News (1983)
Circle The Sun (2025)

Live Albums

BBC Radio Live In Concert '72 (1993)
Devil's Answer 1970-81 BBC Radio (1998)
Live And Raw 1970-71 (2000)
Live In Germany 1983 (2000)
Live At The Marquee 1980 (2002)
Live In London 1972 (2011)
Little Live Rooster (2017)
I Have To Be Free (2024)

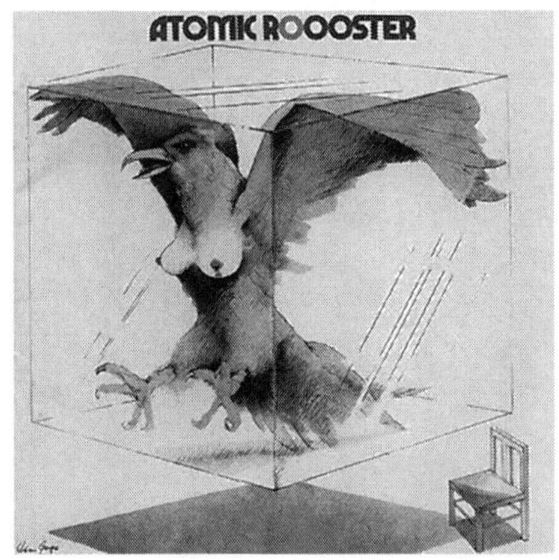

IN HEARING OF
ATOMIC ROOSTER

ATOMIC ROOSTER

ATOMIC ROOSTER
NICE 'N' GREASY

ATOMIC

HEADLINE NEWS
ATOMIC ROOSTER

Compilation Albums

Assortment (1973)
Home To Roost (1977)
The Devil Hits Back (1989)
Castle Masters Collection (1990)
Space Cowboy (1991)
The Best Of Atomic Rooster Vols. 1 And 2 (1992)
In Satan's Name: The Definitive Collection (1997)
The First 10 Explosive Years (1999)
Rarities (2000)
The First 10 Explosive Years Vol. 2 (2001)
Heavy Soul (2001)
Masters From The Vaults (2002)
The Ultimate Chicken (2002)
Lose Your Mind (2005)
Rebel With A Cause (2005)
Close Your Eyes: A Collection 1965-86 (2008)
(Released under the name Vincent Crane)
Homework (2008)
A Classic History Of Atomic Rooster (2018)

Box Sets

Resurrection (2001)
Devil's Answer: The Singles Collection (2001)
(6 x 7" 45s, the five singles released between 1970 and 1973 plus the Crane / Farlowe single.)

Selected Vincent Crane Releases

Singles

Can't Find A Reason / Moods (1973)
(A-side joint Crane/Farlowe track. B-side solely credited to Vincent Crane.)

Fire Fighter / Crazy 'Bout My Baby (1977)
(By Green Goddess)

Albums

Faster Than The Speed Of Light (1979)
(Vincent Crane / Arthur Brown collaboration)

A Case For The Blues / Katmandu (1985)
(By Peter Green with keyboards by Vincent Crane)

Don't Stand Me Down (1985)
(By Dexy's Midnight Runners)

Taro Rota (1997)
(Vincent Crane / Arthur Brown collaboration)

They're With The Band

Atomic Rooster is often remembered as a band defined by its consistency in inconsistency.

Over the course of its existence, there have reportedly been eighteen different line-ups to date, with various musicians serving tenures ranging from a few years to, in some cases, little more than a fleeting visit — just long enough for a quick spot of tea.

What follows is a guide to the band's ever-changing roster: name and time spent in the band. Simple as that.

Current line-up

Steve Bolton (1971-1972/2016-Present)
Shug Millidge (2016-Present)
Adrian Gautrey (2017-Present)
Paul Everett (2020-Present)

Former members

Vincent Crane (1969-1975/1980-1983)
Carl Palmer (1969-1970)
Nick Graham (1969-1970)
John Du Cann (1970-1971/1980-1982)
Ric Parnell (1970/1971-1974)
Paul Hammond (1970-1971/1980-1983)
Pete French (1971/2016-2023)
Chris Farlowe (1972-1974)
Johnny Mandala (John Goodsall) (1972-1974)
Wilgar Campbell (1973)
Geoff Dixon (1973)
Sam Sampson (1974-1975)
Andy Johnson (1974-1975)
Denny Barnes (1974-1975)
Bob Rennie (1974-1975)
Lee Baxter Hayes (1974-1975)
Preston Heyman (1980)
Ginger Baker (1980)

Mick Hawsworth (1981)
John McCoy (1982-1983)
John Mizarolli (1983)
Christian Madden (2016-2017)
Bo Walsh (2016-2020)

Sources

Interviews
Steve Bolton, Bo Walsh, Ginette Baker

Books
Atomic Rooster Complete Recordings

Magazines
Beat Instrumental
Record World
Record Collector
Classic Rock
Progressive Rock Journal

Newspapers
Western Daily Press
East Kent Times And Mail
Northern Echo (North Durham edition)
Surrey Advertiser County Times
Esher News and Mail
Cobham News and Mail
Stoke-on-Trent Evening Sentinel
Evening Standard
Dayton Journal Herald
Los Angeles Times
San Antonio Express and News
Deseret News
Lancaster Telegraph
The Daily Mail
Sounds
Melody Maker
New Musical Express
Black Country Evening Mail
The Independent

Websites

T. Make World.com
The Afterword
Rock Keyboard.com
Garage Hangover.com
The Strange Brew.com
Psychedelic Baby.com
Psychedelic Scene.com
Songfacts.com
Setlist Of Atomic Rooster Tour Statistics.com
Musoscribe.com
Drummer World.com
All Music.com
Perfect Sound Forever.com
Durious.com
Music Without Borders.com
British Occult Society.com
Hit Channel.com
Steve Hoffman's Music Forums.com
Jeannie Crane Home Page.com
Angel Fire.com
Lycos.com
The Sludge Lord.com
Culture Court.com
Prog Archives.com
The Vinyl Hunters.com